How to
MASTER
PSYCHOMETRIC
TESTS

'Every man is like every other man, like some other men, like no other man.'

Clyde Kluckhohn, Anthropologist

How to
MASTER
PSYCHOMETRIC
TESTS

Mark Parkinson

KOGAN
PAGE

YOURS TO HAVE AND TO HOLD

BUT NOT TO COPY

First published in 1997
Reprinted 1997

Kogan Page Limited
120 Pentonville Road
London N1 9JN

© Mark Parkinson, 1997

British Library Cataloguing in Publication Data

A CIP record for this book is available from the British Library.

ISBN 0 7494 2254 8

Typeset by Saxon Graphics Ltd, Derby
Printed in England by Clays Ltd, St Ives plc

Contents

To the Reader

Psychometric tests of ability and personality are used by many organisations throughout the world for selecting people for jobs. They are also used within companies to help with development and promotion.

This book is about preparing you for the main types of tests and increasing your chances of getting to the next stage, the job interview. This is a vital step in the selection process when you consider that 50 per cent or more people fail the tests they take.

All of the tests described in this book are commonly used for recruitment purposes. My job has been to explain what they measure, what they look like, who they are used to assess and how to approach the questions. Importantly the focus is *not* on completing practice questions, as there are many good books which contain these, but on developing an effective test-taking strategy – a personal approach which you can apply to any new test you might encounter.

I also concentrate on the psychological preparation for tests, and how to put yourself in a positive and winning frame of mind. This is just as important to test performance as understanding how the actual questions work.

In short this book gives you the direct practical advice you need to face any test session with confidence.

Mark Parkinson
Berkshire, 1997

Introduction

If you were a personnel manager how would you select new staff?

Probably you would place a job advert and ask people to send a curriculum vitae (CV), or to complete an application form. Then you might look at the forms and invite, depending on how many people applied, between 6 and 12 people to come for an interview. After the interviews, or maybe at the same time, you would follow up references on the best candidates. If this is all you would do, you would be ignoring a technique which has become an essential part of the modern selection process – the psychometric test.

Application forms or CVs are an exercise in seeing how well an applicant, or frequently an agency, can fill in a form or design a work history. Interviews are an example of how prepared a candidate is for a number of standard questions, and of appearing to be interested and motivated for a short period of time. The reference, *at worst*, damns with faint praise, even if the subject has previously been an entirely unsatisfactory employee. In contrast psychometric tests can identify objectively where your abilities lie, and what sort of personality you have. So as long as the appropriate tests are used, they can provide a fair and accurate way of helping to pick the best person for the job.

Tests are also desirable because not everyone is a good interview candidate, but many may still be ideal candidates for the job; and application forms are sometimes so badly designed that it is difficult to present yourself in a positive light. Conversely, skilled CV authors or interviewees may be quite hopeless when they actually secure a position. What this means is that in most circumstances it is to the applicant's *and* employer's advantage that tests are used.

To cut a long story short, what employers want to know is whether you can do a particular job and if you will fit in to an existing workplace. This has more to do with your potential abilities and personality than the number of examination passes you have, or whether you liked going to school or college. Since tests are probably the most efficient way of assessing these factors, it should come as no surprise to discover that most medium to large-sized organisations now use this method of selection.

So, in reality, when you apply for a job, whether this is through a job agency, cold canvassing, an advert in a newspaper or via details held on a website (recruitment information on the WorldWide Web), the next step for the 'successful' candidate is frequently a series of psychometric tests.

Which tests are used?

In the UK, USA and many European countries the most popular tests are those of general intelligence, verbal and numerical ability, and personality. General intelligence tests are concerned with how well you can solve problems from first principles; verbal and numerical tests with aspects of verbal and numerical comprehension, and problem solving; and personality questionnaires with attributes like how outgoing you are, your degree of anxiety or emotionality, mental toughness and personal organisation.

In the UK, if you are invited to attend a test session you will find yourself taking the sort of tests just described. This will be true of virtually all the major retail, manufacturing and service companies, as well as government and some educational and non-profit making organisations. Indeed, over 70 per cent of the *Times Top 1000* companies use tests of this nature. The picture is similar if you apply for jobs in many European Community countries, although some supplement testing with other techniques. For example in France about 60 per cent of the top companies use tests, but 80 per cent also use graphology or handwriting analysis! The same is true in Germany, while around 60 per cent of firms use 'assessment centres', which include tests, interviews and other exercises; great weight is still placed on application forms and reference checks.

Make no mistake, tests are here to stay, so it makes sense to prepare yourself thoroughly for what has become a routine part of the job application process.

About this book

The first chapter of this book looks at the concept of psychometric testing. It explores the different types of tests, and the ways in which they measure both maximum and typical performance. The idea of 'intelligence' is introduced, as well as the differences between tests which measure knowledge (attainment) and potential (aptitude). An explanation of what makes a 'good' test is given, and also how we know that tests actually work. The chapter concludes with details on what employers do with test results, and the different ways in which they can be used to select candidates for jobs.

The next chapter explains the testing process and takes you through a typical selection scenario. This includes the basics of test preparation, and includes what you need to consider before a test session. The problems of test-taking anxiety ('examination nerves') are explained, and a number of methods of reducing anxiety are provided. Additional advice is given on preparing physically and emotionally for tests; and what to do if you have eyesight, hearing or other problems.

Chapter 3 covers, in separate sections, tests of abstract (logical), verbal, numerical, perceptual (diagrammatic), spatial and mechanical ability. The nature and purpose of each type of test is explained, and a number of examples are provided. An explanation of how to approach and to solve each example question is given. Each section also includes information on the sort of candidates who would face each test, eg if you are a graduate the sort of tests you would be asked to complete. Some practical hints are included for each type of test. The chapter concludes with ten additional ways to improve test performance.

Chapter 4 concentrates on the ideas behind personality assessment, and describes the two main models which underpin personality questionnaires. These are the 'type' approach which emphasises preferences for different sorts of behaviour; and the 'trait' school which concentrates on direction and 'quantity' of personality. Extensive details on the format of 'self-report' questionnaires are included, as well as information on how different questionnaires are used. A list of hints for improving performance is provided, such as how to decide what an employer is looking for, and how to assume the correct 'test' taking attitude. Finally, other self-report questionnaires, such as those which measure values, motivation, integrity and interests, are explained.

Chapter 5 provides advice on how to achieve a positive and optimistic frame of mind, and details ways of motivating yourself for the test session. This is of central importance because having sufficient personal confidence frequently makes the difference between success and failure.

The appendices contain useful information on 'competencies', or the work attributes which tests are designed to measure; plus an example of the sort of exercise used by employers simultaneously to assess a group of job applicants. An employer's 'code of conduct', and a list of UK and US test publishers, is also included, with details of websites where appropriate.

In conclusion, this book is about helping you to understand the sort of psychometric tests which you may be asked to complete. It also includes details on how to prepare for tests and what to do if you are nervous about the testing process. The main sections deal with the most popular ability tests and personality questionnaires, and provide up-to-date information on:

- what different types of test measure;
- when they are used in selection;
- what the questions look like;
- how to answer typical questions;
- successful strategies and approaches.

The idea is to give you a set of practical tools which will boost your chances of achieving test and career success. In this way *How to Master Psychometric Tests* will appeal to all those seeking employment with organisations that use tests. It will also be valuable to those who are tested while working within an organisation for development or promotional purposes; and to employers, personnel and human resource professionals unfamiliar with psychometric tests, but who want to know more about what they are and how they can be used.

Note: Masculine pronouns are used in this book to avoid awkward grammatical constructions. In most cases, feminine pronouns can be used interchangeably.

Chapter 1

What are Psychometric Tests?

A psychometric test is a standard way of measuring an aspect of mental performance. Practically this means that tests assess things like verbal ability, such as how good you are at understanding the meaning of words, or comprehending the information in a written passage. They are also used to explore personal attributes like personality or temperament, careers or employment interests, values, attitudes and motivation.

The fact that tests are *standard* methods of assessment is extremely important, and is what makes them different from the 'Personality' and 'Check your own Intelligence' quizzes found in magazines. Psychometric tests are different because everyone is presented with the same questions and instructions for completing them. Crucially, tests are also administered under carefully controlled and timed conditions by a trained individual, who additionally follows precise instructions for scoring and interpreting the results. In this way there is no room for subjectivity, and everyone is treated in exactly the same way. Furthermore, the results a person achieves are compared with a representative sample of people (the normative group) who have completed the test before. This allows a psychologist or personnel professional to decide accurately how well a person has done compared to everyone else. Is the person above or below average? How much is the person above or below?

These features of psychometric tests are also what distinguish them from most forms of examinations. It's true that examinations are timed and that everyone attempts the same paper, but there are usually a variety of questions to choose from. In an essay-based exam it is also the case that there are a number of possible answers to the questions. Clearly some answers will be better than others, and so there are a range of marks on offer. The marking system obviously has to reflect these differences, and so cannot but fail to reflect some of the personal preferences of the examiner. All of this makes most examinations rather less objective than a well-constructed psychometric test.

Personality questionnaires differ in a number of ways from ability tests simply because there are no 'right' or 'wrong' answers. After all there is no such thing as a 'good' or 'bad' personality, just a variety of personal characteristics which may be more or less useful depending on what you are trying to do. However, despite the nature of what is being measured, personality questionnaires still contain questions which everyone must answer; and are administered, scored and interpreted in a standard way.

Different Types of Tests

For most purposes psychologists distinguish between two broad types of tests. The first type is concerned with measuring maximum performance, or how well you can do something. This means that they measure what you know, or what your potential might be, when you are trying to do as well as you can.

The second type of test measures typical performance. In consequence these are concerned with finding out what you are like in normal, day-to-day situations. For instance, are you outgoing and sociable, or do you prefer your own company? Personality questionnaires are an example of this second sort of test, and are particularly useful in those situations where job performance is dependent on how you present yourself to other people, eg all forms of selling activity.

Returning to tests of maximum performance, we find that practically all the ability tests you will be asked to complete as part of a selection process fall in to this category. To be even more precise they can also be classified as follows:

- general intelligence tests;
- attainment tests; and
- aptitude tests.

General intelligence tests

Some tests are formulated so that they measure your overall ability to succeed in a particular activity. These are known as general intelligence tests and are designed to produce a single indication of your ability. This is similar to the concept of the intelligence quotient or IQ. Although in the case of IQ tests the results are expressed in terms of the ratio of your mental age (as measured by a test) to your chronological age, with the resultant multiplied by 100. Thus, if your mental and chronological age are the same you end up with the average IQ of 100. All tests of this sort operate on the principle that your 'general intelligence' affects all of your individual abilities. So, for example, it's your overall intelligence which makes you good or bad at things like verbal or numerical problem solving.

Attainment tests

Attainment tests measure your ability to use the knowledge or skills you already possess. So, if you like, they are designed to assess what you know at the time of the test. For example, can you understand a simple electrical circuit, or do you know the name of the second highest mountain in the world? However, you could ask yourself whether this really is 'typical' performance in the sense of the ability you will bring to a job. Also most attainment tests demand a knowledge of things which may not generalise to every aspect of a job.

Some attainment tests are described as mastery tests. These are based on specific tasks which directly relate to a particular work activity. They are also characterised by the fact that there are only two outcomes; you either 'pass' or 'fail'. The driving test is an example, because you either pass and are permitted to drive a car on the road, or you fail and have to take the test again. Most professional examinations are also mastery tests. This is a sensible thing if you imagine the chaos that would ensue if there were different pass grades for something like medical or dental examinations. Would you go to a particular doctor or dentist if you knew he had only just managed to pass his exams ?

Another sort of attainment test it's useful to know about is the work sample test. These are tests based on the things you actually do in a particular job. For instance, giving someone a typing test which involves measuring their ability to type a dictated letter accurately is a work sample test. Another example is the 'in-tray' or 'in-basket' exercise used in executive assessment centres. This involves presenting a candidate with a number of letters, faxes, e-mails, reports, computer print-outs, invoices and other pieces of information, and asking for them to be put in order of priority and actioned accordingly. This is a highly stressful test maybe, but one that does simulate the work required of many managers.

The most advanced form of work sample test is the aircraft simulator. This allows skills to be assessed, and training to take place, in a safe and cost-effective manner. In fact modern simulators are so realistic that most, if not all, basic training can take place without the pilot ever leaving the hangar. Indeed, legend has it that at least one airline has used pilots who have done all of their advanced training on the ground!

Aptitude tests

Aptitude tests measure your 'natural' ability to do things. Unlike attainment tests they do not require specialist knowledge or skills. Obviously some understanding is involved, if only to comprehend the instructions, but as far as possible the results are designed to reflect your potential to achieve in the future. This makes the aptitude test a fairer assessment for anyone who lacks traditional school qualifications; or who just hasn't had the opportunity to acquire specific skills.

Aptitude tests are frequently used for careers counselling, and also form a useful tool for any employer who wishes to identify potential. Like work-related measures many aptitude tests are constructed so that they indicate whether a person is suitable for a particular job, eg computer programming. However, in contrast to the work sample approach, they do not assume that you have a range of existing skills. The argument is that if you have the potential you can be taught to write programs, calculate exchange rates, compose a technical report, or whatever. Naturally there is also a counter-argument which suggests that aptitude tests do not relate to real job tasks and do not measure experience. This is an interesting point and one which highlights the essential difference between the attainment and aptitude approaches.

You might have noticed in the descriptions of attainment and aptitude tests that they seem to relate to specific abilities. That's because, in contrast to the general intelligence approach, they rely on the idea of different types of intelligence. In many ways this is a far more useful approach because it recognises the fact that we all have different combinations of abilities. It also recognises that one factor, general intelligence, does not dictate everything we can do.

As you might expect, some psychologists believe in the general intelligence approach, and others in the existence of many separate, specific abilities. However, in the real world of work it is usually your specific abilities, whether they be attainment or aptitude based, which are measured in a test session.

What is a 'Good' Test?

Whatever sort of test is used to assess someone for a job it must fulfil a number of important requirements. From the employer's point of view it should obviously be cost-effective, relevant to the position in question, and fair on the people applying. Even more importantly, the test, or tests, must actually work. This depends on the standard administration and objective scoring mentioned earlier, but, even more crucially, on any tests being reliable and valid.

Reliability is all about getting consistent results over time. For example, if I tested you today, and then again in four weeks' time, I would expect to get more or less the same results. I wouldn't expect your abilities to have changed, unless you had learnt something in the interim; or, indeed, for something like your personality to have altered significantly. However, being reliable is not enough because it is possible to achieve consistent results and still not be measuring anything meaningful. A good example is the 'buttercup test' we used as children.

If you hold a buttercup under your chin on a sunny day it will cast a yellow shadow. This is supposed to indicate a liking for butter. However, as you will no doubt appreciate, if it's sunny you will always get a yellow spot on your chin. It's a very reliable test, but unfortunately there is no real link between yellow shadows and butter appreciation.

Clearly it's not enough for a test to be reliable, it must be valid as well. Indeed validity, or the extent to which a test measures what the designer says it's measuring, is the most fundamental attribute of any measure. However, validity is rather a complicated thing to establish, and to confuse things further there are a number of different types.

For example, face validity refers to the extent to which a test measures what it looks as if it's measuring. For example, if a test is designed to assess numerical ability you would expect it to contain mathematical problems. You would not expect it to have a lot of highly verbal items, or ask you about how you prefer to socialise with other people.

While face validity is important it does not guarantee that a test works (think about the magazine 'tests' mentioned at the beginning of this chapter); so it's important to establish what is known as criterion-related validity. This is also sometimes called external validity and is the degree to which a test correlates with another measure of the same thing. For instance, you might expect a numerical test to correlate with mathematical ability, as measured by a formal examination. Yet, important as this might be, the ultimate sort of external validity is predictive validity. This sort of validity is when we can demonstrate that a test predicts a future measure of performance. Put simply, if I give you a particular test, can I say that if you achieve a certain score there is an increased chance of you being a more productive employee?

To summarise what we have learnt in this chapter so far, a 'good' test should be as follows.

- **Objective.** Each person who takes it should be treated in exactly the same way. The scoring and interpretation of the results should be conducted according to the directions laid down by the test designer.
- **Standardised.** The score a person gets on the test should be compared against a representative group of people who have taken the test in the past (the normative group). Any decisions should then only be made in comparison with this standard group.
- **Reliable.** The test must consistently measure the same thing, with no marked differences over time. The exception, of course, is where we use an attainment test and wish to measure what you have learnt over a period of time.
- **Predictive.** The test must be a valid measure of what it's supposed to measure. It is also important to establish that it's an accurate predictor of how someone will perform in the future.
- **Unbiased.** The test should only measure an aspect of maximum or typical performance. It should not discriminate in terms of race, culture, gender or any similar factor. Naturally there may

be differences between different groups, but these must only be due to actual differences in ability or personality, and not just a product of the way a test is worded or constructed.

Considering these requirements it should now be obvious that writing a test is a complex process, and perhaps not the 'armchair' exercise many people imagine it to be. Then again, the fact that 'good' tests conform to all these requirements should be a comfort to the potential test taker. After all tests are used to assess people for one of life's most taxing environments – the workplace.

How are Test Results Used?

There are a number of ways in which test results can be used to assess people. However, the prime objective of all these methods is to identify at an early stage those job applicants who are unlikely to fill the requirements of the position on offer. They do this by providing a scientific benchmark against which all applicants can be assessed. In this way ability test results can be used to supply information on current knowledge or performance; and personality questionnaires the sort of insights that are difficult to achieve in a 45 to 60-minute interview.

A warning should be sounded at this point because while what has just been said is correct, the usefulness of any testing process depends on knowing exactly what you are looking for in the first place. This depends on a comprehensive analysis of the job, or jobs, in question. It's only after the personnel professional or psychologist has established a specification for a job that meaningful comparisons can be made. Thus in the normal course of events information is gathered on the following.

- **Knowledge.** Is a specialist sort of knowledge required? For example, do you need an in-depth understanding of legal terms and procedures?
- **Skills.** Are particular skills crucial to good performance? For example, are certain computer or IT (information technology) skills essential?
- **Abilities.** Are particular underlying abilities considered necessary? For example, do you need an aptitude for verbal or numerical problem solving?

- **Experience.** Is a certain type or range of experience valuable? For example, is experience of doing business in different countries required?

Sometimes these different sorts of job requirements are combined in to what are called competencies. These are 'clusters' of abilities, experience and knowledge, and are frequently the things asked for in job advertisements. For example, an advert may demand leadership skills, creativity, persuasiveness and planning ability. If you want to know more about competencies, a list, with definitions, is provided in Appendix 1 to this book.

After the job analysis and the testing, the first step is to compare the results against the appropriate normative group. The findings can then be expressed in a number of ways, but one of the commonest is to describe the overall results in terms of percentiles. For example, if you score at the 70th percentile it means that you have done better than 70 per cent of the population; or, to put it another way, you are in the top 30 per cent.

The next step involves taking one of three approaches. The first approach is called 'top-down' selection. As the name implies this means that you select the top scorers, from the highest downwards, until you have filled all your positions. However, there can be problems, for example what happens if all the test takers actually got relatively low scores? In reality none of them may be particularly good prospects. Also, if you only select from the top scores, you might recruit people who are too high powered for the job in question. This is a real danger and was a mistake made in the 1980s by a number of major UK banks. The end result was a rapid and expensive turnover of staff as a result of their boredom.

An alternative approach is to use a 'minimum cut-off' technique. This relies on setting a minimum level for a test, or tests, above which candidates have to score. The level is usually established by testing existing employees, and is set at the point which represents satisfactory performance. But, as with the top-down approach, there can be difficulties, especially if the job is a new one. How can you set a standard for a job no one else is doing? It also relies on existing personnel being willing to be tested, and clearly on them actually being good performers in the first place! However, all other things being equal, this is still a very popular approach.

The last way of dealing with test results is to concentrate on profiles. What this means is that if a number of tests have been taken it is possible to look at the 'shape' of the results. In this way the psychologist or personnel manager can see the relative strengths and weaknesses of an applicant. For example, many administrative jobs require greater verbal and numerical ability than they do perceptual ability (understanding diagrams). This difference is obvious if the relative levels of test results are compared. Once this initial assessment is made the minimum requirements on individual tests can then be considered.

The profile approach is the most complex, but probably also the fairest of them all. However, as it takes more time than straight 'top-down' or 'minimum cut-off' approaches, it tends to be used less.

What Influences Test Performance?

There are many techniques you can use to improve your test results, and these are covered in the chapters which follow. However, there are some factors you cannot control and which will inevitably influence how you perform in a test situation. These include things like age, gender and health, and also your educational, ethnic and home background.

As we get older some of our mental faculties tend to decline. For example, if you measure general intelligence you find that the peak ages are from about 15 years old to the mid-20s. After that it's downhill all the way! But before you get too depressed this does not apply to all abilities, and general knowledge and experience increase with age. Personality also tends to stabilise with age, and the older you get the better you are at coping with your own personality.

Your gender can also influence your test performance. It's a fact that women do less well, on average, on tests of mechanical and spatial ability. These are tests which measure how good you are at understanding basic mechanical principles, and at imagining objects in three dimensions. However, to even up the balance, women frequently do better than men on tests of speed and accuracy. On average, this time, they are quicker and more precise in what they do.

If you are unwell at the time you do a test this will affect your performance. For example, if you have a temperature or just feel generally below par, it's unlikely that you will be able to do your best. Other long-lasting conditions such as anything which affects the movement of your hands, wrists and arms will also tend to interfere with your test-taking ability, especially how quickly you can work. This is important because many of the tests you will encounter will have strict time limits.

Aspects of where you come from, the standard of your education, your ethnic origin, and your home environment can also influence how you do. For example, if you didn't do very well at school, or just didn't like it, it's probable that your results on attainment tests will be lower than they could be. Conversely, if you come from a home environment where study and reading were encouraged, this will probably increase your chances of getting better results.

Another very important factor is your ability with the English language. This can make a real difference because if English is your second, or even your third, language, you will be at a disadvantage in most tests. The reason is that the vast majority of tests are only available in English, and if you have to think in your native language and then translate answers into English it will significantly slow your progress. The end result will be lower marks again because tests operate within strict time limits.

In conclusion what we are really talking about is opportunity, and if there are any factors which reduced your exposure to good education and learning, these will have an effect.

Key Points

- A psychometric test is a standard and scientific way of assessing an aspect of human performance or behaviour.
- Tests measure things like general intelligence, attainment, aptitude and personality. They can also measure attitudes, interests, values and what motivates you.
- Tests are constructed so that they are objective, reliable, valid and unbiased. A great deal of effort is put in to making them a fair way of assessing people.
- Tests results are used to assess people against the requirements for a job. Jobs are usually specified in terms of the knowledge, skills, abilities and the experience required to do them.
- Tests results are interpreted by comparing them against a stan-

dard group of people who have done the test in the past (the normative group).

- Decisions are made by applying one of a number of techniques. The most common approaches are 'top-down' and 'minimum cut-off' selection, or profiling.
- There are many factors which can influence your performance on a test. These include age, gender and health, and all aspects of your personal background.

Chapter 2

Preparing for Psychometric Tests

When you apply for a job your application form or CV is compared against the requirements for that job. If you fulfil the initial requirements, in terms of things like qualifications and experience, you may then be asked to attend a test session. This session is designed to fill in some of the gaps, to provide additional information on your abilities and, more often than not, your personality.

The test session is usually scheduled for about seven to ten days after all the applications have been processed, and is marked by a letter of invitation. In the letter you will be told about the time and place of the session, how to get there, and any other points that might be important. Some employers will also include a practice test which will explain why the test, or tests, are being used; how you might benefit from the testing process, and what the questions will look like. Indeed most practice tests include a number of questions for you to attempt and, of course, the answers. The purpose of practice tests is to give everyone an equal chance and, importantly, to give some practice material to those who have not done tests before.

A typical letter of invitation looks like this:

Mr D. Grayson
12 Oak Tree Avenue
Longton
East Middleshire
EM12 4TX

[Date]

Dear Mr Grayson

Administration Manager Position

Thank you for applying for the position of Administration Manager in our Holytown store. We have now assessed all the applications and would like to invite you to a psychometric testing session to be held at the Holytown store on 18 May at 9:30 am. You will find a map and details of car parking attached. If you are coming by train the nearest station is Holytown Riverside, on the Eastern Line.
The test session will last for two hours with a short break in the middle. You will be asked to complete two tests of ability, and a personality questionnaire. To give you an idea of what to expect we have enclosed a practice paper. If you read the instructions and answer the questions it will help you understand what the tests are measuring, and what the real test questions will look like.
You do not need to bring any pens, writing materials, or a pocket calculator to the test session, as everything will be provided. However, if you normally wear reading glasses make sure you bring them with you. Also, if you are going to find it difficult to go for two hours without anything to eat or drink, remember that there will be a break in the middle when refreshments will be provided.
Please let me know as soon as possible if you can attend this session. If you have any questions contact my assistant, John Blake, on Holytown 339978. I look forward to meeting you on 18 May.
Yours sincerely,

Jenny Munroe
Human Resources Manager
Triangle Stores Group

Coping with Test Anxiety

The prospect of being tested fills many people with anxiety. Indeed, even those who are used to formal tests and examinations are likely to suffer from at least some degree of nervousness. This is all perfectly natural and is a consequence of the importance of the situation, where a job may depend on your performance; and the unknown elements of the testing process. Practice tests, if they are used, are designed to help with the last point, but even so there is still room for the imagination to do its worst!

The first thing to appreciate is that a certain degree of anxiety actually improves performance. The trick is to manage it, and to make sure that it does not reach an unacceptable level. You will know if it's unacceptable because you will start to show some of the classic physical and behavioural signs of stress. These include the following.

Physical signs

- General fatigue
- Sleeplessness
- Headaches
- Back or shoulder ache
- Upset stomach.

Behavioural signs

- Irritability
- Loss of concentration
- Depression
- Change in appetite (eating more *or* less than usual)
- Drinking or smoking more
- Feelings of panic.

Before you get too worried, there are effective ways of controlling all of these stress symptoms. By far the best is to know what to expect, and this is what this chapter and the rest of the book is about. It's also important immediately to control unwanted and irrational thoughts, and to dismiss notions such as:

- Tests confuse me.
- My mind will go blank.

- I can never remember anything.
- I always go to pieces.
- I always run out of time.
- My memory will let me down.
- I'm stupid, I won't be able to do it ...

As any counsellor or psychologist would point out, having these thoughts does not make them happen. They are just a reflection of the performance anxiety you feel before a test session. The key is to keep everything in proportion and not to start to believe what are frequently completely unrealistic personal 'predictions'. It's very unlikely to be a complete disaster, your family will not disown you; and if the worst comes to the worst, there are always other opportunities.

Practically, you need to get yourself into good mental and physical shape for a test session. This means getting enough sleep, eating and drinking properly, and making sure that you have taken enough exercise. If you're going to prepare for tests by working through practice questions or specialist books, do not stay up all night studying. Let's face it, it's very unlikely that you will do your best if you are tired, hungry and pumped full of caffeine!

You will also find it useful to build in periods of formal relaxation to your daily timetable. These may include any sort of activities which help you to unwind, and perhaps one of a number of special methods of stress reduction. Strategies such as these are important if you're presently unemployed and looking for a job, and also if you already have one and wish to move to a new position.

The two methods of stress reduction it is useful to know about are simple body relaxation and visualisation. Both these approaches have proven ability to reduce anxiety levels and to make taking tests a less stressful process. They can be practised in the days leading up to the test session, and while waiting to go in to the test room itself.

Simple body relaxation

This is a technique which will help you to relax your muscles in sequence from your feet to your head, taking in your legs, thighs, chest, shoulders, arms, neck and head. It's a classic method and is very effective in calming the body, and reducing feelings of stress and anxiety. Interestingly, it is also a technique which is taught to people who want to learn about self-hypnosis. However, in saying this, do not worry about putting yourself into a trance. If you are tired to start with the most that will happen is that you will fall asleep.

The sequence of instructions is easy to remember and you can practise relaxing yourself at any time when you have ten minutes or so to spare. All you need is a quiet room which is at a comfortable temperature, where you are unlikely to be disturbed. Prior to a test session you can achieve the same results by sitting quietly with your eyes closed, silently working through the instructions in your head.

To relax your body work through the following steps. Concentrate on your:

- **toes**   tense the muscles in your toes, and then relax;
- **feet**   tense the muscles in both your feet, and then relax;
- **lower legs**   tense your lower leg muscles, and then relax;
- **thighs**   tense your thigh muscles, and then relax;
- **stomach and lower back**   tense the muscles, and then relax;
- **chest**   tense the muscles in your chest, and then relax;
- **shoulders**   tense your shoulder muscles, and then relax;
- **upper arms**   tense the muscles in your upper arms, and then relax;
- **lower arms and hands**   tense all the muscles and then relax;
- **neck**   tense your neck muscles, and then relax;
- **head**   tense your head muscles (frown!), and then relax.

If you follow this sequence you should feel a warm wave of relaxation spreading up your body. It should help you to feel comfortable and less anxious. If you only have time to follow a shorter sequence just concentrate on your shoulders, neck and head. Systematically tensing and relaxing just these muscle groups will make quite a difference. Finally, remember that if you want to try this technique immediately before a test session you can always use the washroom.

Visualisation

This technique, also known as 'mental picturing', is designed to put you in a positive frame of mind. It's routinely used by sports professionals as it also has the effect of focusing the attention on the task at hand.

The idea is to put yourself in to a daydream state and to imagine success. In this case you imagine the successful and satisfactory completion of a test session. It works because it has been found that repeatedly picturing something, clearly and vividly, acts on the unconscious mind. In fact the mind begins to believe the 'dream', and starts to mobilise resources to make it a reality. At the same time, because your mind is focused on a successful outcome, you do not have time to worry.

In order to use visualisation to help you prepare for a test session you need to do the following:

- Make yourself comfortable. You can do this by using the progressive body relaxation technique described earlier. Alternatively you can just settle yourself down in a warm, quiet room and empty your mind of extraneous thoughts – try focusing on something in front of you, a plant or an object maybe, and letting any thoughts you have drift away.
- Check that you feel relaxed. Mentally run round your body and make sure that no particular part is feeling tense. If it is, concentrate on that part and relax the muscles.
- Think about a time when you were successful at something. Remember the feeling of success, the euphoria at having achieved something worth-while. Imagine doing the same thing again, and the pleasant feelings which went with it. Try and visualise yourself passing that examination; winning the sports competition; signing the big contract – whatever has made you feel proud and successful. Hold on to the positive and warm thoughts you are having …
- Now visualise yourself waiting outside the test room feeling confident. You are well prepared, *you know what to expect*. You enter the room and sit in your place. On the table in front of you are some test books and answer papers, *as you anticipated*. You look around the room at the other candidates. You feel confident and know that you are just as well, if not better, prepared, than anyone else there. The test administrator introduces the session and *tells you what to expect*. The session starts and you carefully read the instructions for the first test. You have prepared yourself for this sort of test, and so you can immediately start on the first question. After the appropri-

ate amount of time has passed the administrator asks you to stop. As you were told how long the test would last you have *budgeted your time accordingly*. More instructions follow, and you *complete* all the remaining tests and questionnaires. At the end of the session you know that you *understood the instructions for all of the tests, and completed every one to the best of your ability*. Hold on to that thought.

- Practise and follow the same pattern of thoughts in the days before the test session, and especially if you start to feel any nervousness or anxiety.

Both body relaxation and visualisation only work if you practise. So think of them as new skills, and make sure that you put some effort in to developing your technique. They really can help you relax, and will put you in a winning frame of mind.

The Test Session

If you were expected to make any particular preparations before the test session these will have been outlined in your letter of invitation. However, it's probably worth mentioning at this point that if you have any special requirements you *must* make sure that the testing organisation knows about them in advance. For example, if you have mobility problems ensure that provision has been made for you to get to the test room. If you have stiff or arthritic hands or wrists, tell them. Remember that many tests are timed and so you will not be able to work as quickly as other people. Also, if you have restricted eyesight, or hearing problems, make sure this is known. Larger print tests are available, and it is possible to 'reserve' a seat in the front row.

A test session is a formal event and so you can always expect the test administrator to explain exactly what is required. The following description covers the main features of *any* selection test administration, and concentrates on those things you need to consider in order to do your best.

In the test room

Tests take place in rooms with desks or tables laid out in rows, and at most sessions you will find yourself being tested with up to 20 other candidates. It is very unlikely that you will be tested by yourself, unless the test(s) are administered by computer.

In most test sessions it does not matter where you sit. However, if you are unsure, always ASK.

The test materials

When you sit down you will typically find a number of test question books, answer sheets, two pencils and an eraser in front of you. You will only be supplied with other items, rough paper or an electronic calculator, for example, if they are essential for any of the tests.

Use the materials provided. Do not use any pens or pencils you may have brought with you. The reason is that many test papers are marked by optical scanning systems, and these work best with pencil marks.

If the test materials do not comprise separate question books and answer sheets they will be in one of the following three formats:

1. A combined question and answer book which allows you to write your answers by the questions.
2. A question book and a 'palm-top' computer. In this arrangement you read the questions in the book and enter your answers using the computer keyboard.
3. A 'palm-top' or personal computer. This time the questions appear on the computer screen and you enter your answers using the keyboard.

In time you will also encounter multi-media tests. These are tests presented on a computer which combine text, sound, video-clips, and movement. In addition there are a number of tests on the WorldWide Web. For example, the UK Civil Service recently placed some practice tests on the Web in conjunction with a newspaper advertisement campaign.

The session introduction

When everyone is settled the test administrator (a personnel assistant, human resources (HR) manager or psychologist) will introduce the session. A typical introduction follows:

'Good morning, I would first like to welcome you to The Triangle Stores Group – TSG. My name is Jenny Munroe and

I am the Human Resources Manager with TSG. I will be organising your activities this morning, and for the rest of your time with us.

Secondly can I just check that you all received the details which we sent to you, and you know what is going to happen to you this morning. You should have received a practice test which covered the verbal and numerical tests you will be completing; and some details on the personality questionnaire. Did you receive the details?

[Any questions are answered]

We use the tests described in your letter because they give a fair and objective view of your abilities and personality. We have found that people who do well on these tests also tend to do well in the job. However, I would just like to assure you that we do take other information into account, in particular your application details.

Before I introduce the tests themselves I would just like to make sure that you are all comfortable and ready to begin. Also, if you would like to visit the washroom, now is a good time. It's out of the door, turn left, through the double doors, and straight ahead. Are there any questions before we begin?

[There is a short break for visits to the washroom and questions]

The test session will last for two hours with a short break in the middle. There will be two tests of ability, verbal and numerical, and a personality questionnaire. I will tell you when to start and stop each test, so please do not open any of the booklets in front of you until you are told to begin.

In order to do your best you need to keep the following points in mind:

- Please ask questions *before* the tests if you do not understand what to do. I can always explain what you need to do again.
- Read the instructions for each test carefully. Don't rush as it's very important you complete the tests in the correct way.
- Work as quickly and as accurately as you can. Remember that there is a time limit for the tests.
- Don't spend too long on any question. If you can't do one, make an informed guess and go on with the next.

- Overall, the more questions you do, the better your chances of getting a higher score.

Do you have any final questions before we begin?'

The tests

The administrator will read out the instructions for each test in turn. These will include details on how to approach the questions and the time allowed. You will also have an opportunity to complete some practice questions and ask any questions yourself.

Make sure you understand the practice questions. If you find them difficult, or just don't know what to do, ASK.

During the test session the administrator watches the candidates and records any events which may affect performance, eg excessive noise or disturbance. The administrator will also make a note if you ask for assistance or, for example, mark your answers on the wrong answer sheet. These factors will be taken into account at the marking stage. For instance, if you do put your answers on the wrong sheet, they will be transferred to the correct form and marked accordingly. It will not put you at a disadvantage.

The end of the session

At the end of the session the administrator will collect all the answer sheets, making sure that none are missing, and that they all have the candidates' names and other details on them. You will be thanked for attending and the next stage of the selection process will be explained. This will normally involve the scoring of the tests and the selection of people for interview.

In many cases tests can be marked very quickly and so interviews can take place on the same day as the testing. While this is happening your time may well be spent on a tour of the site or premises, or having lunch. After this period the 'successful' candidates will be invited to stay for interview.

If you are unsuccessful always ask if you can have some feedback on your test results.

A knowledge of your results will be invaluable for any further applications you make. Most companies are happy to give feedback, although it may only be at a later date and over the telephone. However, it's still going to be useful information about your test performance in a real selection situation.

Countdown to Test-Day

In the lead up to a test session make sure you learn as much as you can about the sort of tests or questionnaires you may be asked to complete. If you are sent a practice test make sure that you try it; and read any other details very carefully. It's also useful to work out exactly where you are expected to go for your tests, how you are going to get there, the time it will take, and so forth. There's nothing more unnerving than getting lost on the way and arriving late. Indeed, if you arrive very late you will *not* be able to take part in the test session.

T-DAY minus 7: the seven days before the test session

- Read all the materials that are sent to you with great care.
- Complete any practice tests supplied and check the answers.
- Use this book, and any other books containing practice questions, to prepare.
- Familiarise yourself with different sorts of test formats and questions.
- If you suffer from pre-test nerves try one of the relaxation techniques recommended earlier.
- Make sure you know *exactly* where, and at what time, the test session is being held.

T-DAY minus 1: the day before the test session

- Keep calm. If you've prepared yourself properly you don't need to panic.
- Review what you know about the tests you will be asked to complete.
- Reduce any tension by using a relaxation technique. Exercise is also a good way of reducing stress – try a brisk 20 minute walk.
- Eat normally. Don't overeat, or be tempted to drink a lot of alcohol, tea or coffee.
- Get a good night's sleep. Don't stay up all night 'cramming', or go out on a date!

T-DAY: the day of the test session

- Eat normally. Even if you don't feel like it have a decent breakfast. This is especially important if you're diabetic and suffer from low blood sugar.

- If you wear reading glasses or a hearing aid make sure you take them with you.
- Take the letter of invitation and the directions.
- Arrive at the test venue in good time. This means at least 15 to 20 minutes before the billed start time.
- Visit the washroom and have a quiet think.
- Make sure you know where to sit in the test room.

During the session

Here are 24 key points for test success:

1. Keep as calm as you can. Remember that a certain amount of anxiety is perfectly normal.
2. Don't show any agitation and don't lose your temper. You need to appear confident because your general behaviour will be under scrutiny as well as your test performance.
3. Make yourself comfortable. Loosen your collar and tie (if appropriate), and kick off your shoes if you need to.
4. Listen carefully to the administrator's instructions. Ask questions if you do not understand anything.
5. If you can't see or hear things properly tell the administrator.
6. Read the test instructions carefully and do not *assume* that you know what to do.
7. Put your answers in the correct place on the answer sheet. If you miss a question out, because you intend to return to it, make sure you do not get out of sequence.
8. Record your answers in the correct way. For example, do *not* tick boxes if you're expected to strike through them with short pencil lines.
9. Read the questions properly before you attempt to answer them.
10. Don't agonise over a question you can't do, but move on to the next one.
11. Don't waste time double-checking questions with easy or obvious answers.
12. Don't waste time looking for 'trick' questions as there won't be any.
13. If you can't work out an answer, make an informed guess.
14. Work as quickly as you can, but don't race or you will make *avoidable* mistakes. For example, it's very easy to reverse numbers and to imagine, say, that an answer is 145 rather than 154.

15. Remember that the more questions you answer the greater your chances of getting a higher mark.
16. Keep an eye on the time. If you have time left at the end of a test go back and check your answers.
17. Don't stick slavishly to a certain amount of time for each question, eg 30 seconds for each question, if there are 60 to complete in half-and-hour. Many tests are designed so that the questions get harder, and so need progressively more time as you go on.
18. If you want any assistance during a test ask the administrator. The administrator won't give you further instructions once the test has started, but will be able to help you with any problems you might have concerning the 'mechanics' of the session, eg not knowing where to write your answers, a defective question book, blunt or broken pencils, no eraser ...
19. Look around occasionally and relax: take some deep breaths, rest your eyes, stretch your legs. This will help to break the tension that will inevitably build up in your body.
20. Don't be put off if the questions seem difficult. They may well be just as difficult for everyone else, and you don't know the pass mark.
21. Don't be alarmed if your neighbours appear to be working much quicker than you. It's no guarantee that their answers are correct!
22. If for any reason you feel unwell tell the administrator. There are no prizes for suffering in silence.
23. Don't be hard on yourself, you can only do your best.
24 Keep a cool head and, if you need help, ask for it.

Chapter 3

Ability Tests

There are about 50 human abilities that can be measured using psychometric tests. These fall into four main categories covering the cognitive abilities such as numerical or verbal reasoning; psychomotor abilities like hand–eye co-ordination; physical abilities relating to stamina and strength; and sensory abilities concerning vision, hearing and speech.

In an assessment context the tests used may be selected from just one of these categories, or from a number. For example, some jobs require verbal and numerical ability; while others demand numerical and perceptual reasoning (understanding diagrams) *and* perfect colour vision. So the task of the personnel specialist can be very complicated because different jobs require different tests, and also because there is a vast range of tests to choose from. In fact there are between 4000 to 5000 tests on the market, with virtually all of them designed for use in English-speaking countries.

This makes the job of preparing for ability tests sound rather overwhelming, but in reality most selection procedures focus on the six main types of cognitive reasoning test:

- abstract;
- verbal;
- numerical;
- perceptual;
- spatial;
- mechanical.

There are other sorts of cognitive tests such as those which assess the ability to check information quickly and accurately. This is an important ability to measure in any job requiring the processing of large quantities of detailed information.

The next section deals with the six main types and provides information on what is being measured, the different sorts of question format, and hints on improving your performance. There is also some guidance on which type and format of test is used to assess which sort of job, along with the names of some of the most commonly used tests.

Abstract Reasoning

Abstract reasoning tests measure general intellectual reasoning ability. This concerns how well you can solve a problem from first principles. It involves identifying the underlying logic of an 'argument' or question.

The questions in this sort of test are usually in the form of sequences of symbols arranged in rows or squares, and in order to solve them you must work through three distinct steps: your first task is to identify the different sorts of symbols, and decide what they have in common. For example, in most tests the differences will include some or all of the following:

- **shape**, eg circles, triangles, squares, rectangles, pentagons, hexagons;
- **size**, eg small, medium and large;
- **colour**, eg the three primary colours;
- **features**, eg the number of circles, lines or points on a star.

Having examined the symbols, and what they have in common, the next step is to identify the pattern. This involves seeing how the symbols are ordered or grouped. For example, are they in repeating patterns of two, three or more symbols? If they are in a square format, does the order go from left to right, right to left, top to bottom, bottom to top, or diagonally?

The last step is to predict the next part of the sequence from what you have learnt about the logic of the pattern.

Example 1: Abstract Reasoning
What are the next two symbols in the sequence?

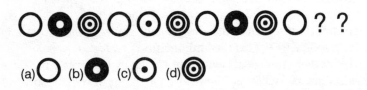

Example 2: Abstract Reasoning
What is the missing symbol?

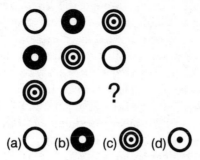

In Example 1 you will see that there are four different types of symbol, all of which are the same size. The (a) symbol always goes immediately after the (d) symbol, leaving the other two to alternate. Since there are two (b)s and only one (c), the next symbols in the sequence must be (c), followed by (d). Likewise in Example 2, it's a question of working out what is happening in each row or column. This one is obviously easier because there are three symbols in use, and they appear in each complete row or column only once. Thus it is logical to assume that the missing symbol is (b). However it's also interesting to note that there is a diagonal sequence which runs (a)–(b)–(c)–(a). This is an important point to grasp because in questions presented as 'squares' there is often more than one way of reaching the correct answer.

Uses

Abstract reasoning tests provide the best single measure of general ability and so are used for all types of jobs at all levels. This means that there is a chance you will have to do this sort of test whatever the job for which you are applying. However, they are obviously of particular value for any job which focuses on the ability to deal with abstract ideas, concepts or theories. Thus they are generally a fixed feature of recruitment to scientific or technological jobs.

The most widely used tests of general intellectual ability are *Raven's Progressive Matrices*, published by Oxford Psychologists Press. Another popular measure is the *Compound Series Test* from The Morrisby Organisation.

Hints

Seek out abstract problems in newspapers, magazines and quiz books, and practice working through the three steps suggested. You may also find it useful to make up your own questions and try them on other people. The action of explaining the answers will help fix in your mind the different ways in which these questions can work. Finally, if you get stuck on a particular question in a test always go back to first principles and identify the component parts of the symbols, and then the pattern. Sometimes it also helps to continue with the other questions and return to a problem question later with a fresh viewpoint. This will stop you becoming fixated on a particular solution.

Verbal Reasoning

Verbal reasoning tests measure your ability to understand and use words. They are concerned with things like spelling, grammar, sentence completion, analogies and following verbal instructions. The more complex verbal tests look at how well you can understand and reason with passages of verbal information. The questions in verbal tests come in many different forms, but they all rely on understanding the meaning of words, and the structure and logic of language.

Example 3: Spelling
Which of the following words are *incorrectly* spelt?
(a) Persistant (b) Separate (c) Success (d) Recieve

Example 4: Grammar
What, if anything, is grammatically *incorrect* with the following sentences?
(a) The elephant was very enormous.
(b) Its unlikely that we can catch the train.
(c) She took the books and the rest of the money off of me.
(d) They should have took the boxes with them.

Example 5: Sentence Completion
Which word best completes the sentence?
(1) The painting, originally .... to a Dutch
artist, is now thought to be by John Constable.
(a) prescribed (b) assigned (c) attributed (d) linked
(e) designated
(2) Our company's name is .... with quality and
    value for money.
(a) connected (b) synonymous (c) aligned (d) concerned
(e) equated

In Example 3 you need to know how to spell a series of everyday words, and (a) and (d) are incorrectly spelt. The trick with Example 4 is to understand some of the principles of English grammar, and to realise that there are errors in all of them! In (a) the word 'very' is not needed, as 'enormous' means 'very large'; in (b), 'Its' should be 'It's'; and in (c) the word 'of' is not required. Finally, in (d), the word 'took' should be 'taken'. In Example 5 the questions are known as 'cloze' tasks, and the idea in each case is to identify the best possible word. Therefore in question (1) the most correct answer is (c), because paintings are 'attributed' to artists; and in (2) the answer is (b), because 'synonymous' means 'closely associated'.

Example 6: Verbal Analogies
Letter is to word as sentence is to:
(a) verb (b) paragraph (c) phrase (d) book?
Over is to under as below is to:
(a) beneath (b) beside (c) above (d) submerged?

Example 7: Word Groups
Which *two* words do not belong with the other four?
(1) (a) stone (b) wood (c) plastic (d) coal (e) nylon (f) gas
(2) (a) trousers (b) hat (c) socks (d) shirt (e) boots (f) shorts

Example 8: Following Instructions
Use the information below to answer the questions. For each question select the correct answer from the five options provided.

Surgery Times

The surgery is now open from 8.30am to 12.30pm, and from 1.00pm to 6.30pm.

There is a late surgery on Tuesdays and Thursdays from 7.30pm. to 10.00pm. If you have a minor surgery appointment please confirm at the beginning of the week, as all procedures are performed on Thursday afternoons. The 'Well Woman' clinic continues to take place on alternate Saturday mornings. The next meeting is scheduled for the 25th of this month, please see the practice nurse for details.

If you have a minor surgery appointment when must you attend?
(a) Normal surgery hours.
(b) Late surgery on Thursday.
(c) The beginning of the week.
(d) Monday or Wednesday morning.
(e) Thursday afternoon.

In Examples 6 and 7 you need to understand directly the meanings and relationships between words. Thus, in Example 6, the answer to the first analogy is (b), because the progression is to bigger units; and in the other analogy the answer is (c) because the starting analogy was one of opposites. Readers should note that in this sort of question there may be *any* relationship between the words, eg:

- **synonyms**, ie words with the same meanings;
- **antonyms**, ie words with opposite meanings;
- **part to whole**, eg 'letter' is to 'word';
- **cause and effect**, eg 'exercise' is to 'fatigue';
- **sequence**, eg 'Summer' is to 'Autumn';
- **degree**, eg: 'hot' is to 'warm';
- **object and action**, eg 'kick' is to 'football';
- **groups**, eg 'red' is to 'green' (other colours).

Indeed, Example 7 is a case of words falling into particular groups. So the answer to (1) is (c) and (e) because they are both man-made, while the other materials are natural; and to (2) it is (b) and d), because they are items of clothing worn above the waist, while the others are worn below. In Example 8 details are given of a doctor's surgery times and the question is designed to discover whether you can understand simple instructions. The answer is actually very straightforward and is (e). However, these sorts of questions can be much more difficult, eg on what date was the last 'Well Woman' clinic?

The most complicated sorts of verbal assessments are called verbal critical reasoning tests. These present you with a short passage of written information followed by a number of statements. The task is to decide whether each statement is 'True' (follows logically from the information provided); 'False' (does not follow logically); or if you 'Cannot Tell', because there is insufficient information. All the information required to make the decision is contained in the passage. However, just to complicate the issue, the information given frequently relates to subjects about which you may already know, or have formed particular opinions

Example 9: Verbal Critical Reasoning
Read the passage and decide if the statements which follow are True, False or if you Cannot Tell.

'Smoking can cause problems in many work environments. In the office it can not only lead to heated arguments, but to health problems as well. Indeed the *New England Journal of Medicine* (NEJM) recently reported that passive smoking, or the involuntary inhalation of other people's smoke, can be a major health hazard. Like regular smokers, it puts passive smokers at an increased risk of developing chest and circulatory diseases.'

1. Smokers are more likely to have heart attacks.
2. Passive smoking means inhaling someone else's smoke.
3. Smoking can make offices calmer places in which to work.

Some verbal critical reasoning tests have more than three answer options, and split the reasoning tasks into a number of types. So, for example, you have to decide if a statement is 'True', 'Probably True', 'False', 'Probably False' or if you 'Cannot Tell'. The questions are then based on different types of logical argument, eg:

- whether deductions (judgements based on general principles) are valid;
- whether inferences (conclusions based on given facts) are accurate;

- whether valid assumptions are being made;
- the strength of verbal arguments;
- whether conclusions based on factual interpretations are valid.

For example, deductions are sometimes based on pairs of logically consistent verbal arguments or 'syllogisms'.

Example 10: Verbal Deductions

'Some animals are venomous. All venomous animals are dangerous to touch.'

Which of the following are valid deductions?

1. All non-venomous animals are safe to touch.
2. Some animals are dangerous.
3. Some animals are safe to touch.

The answers to Example 9 are (1), 'Cannot Tell'; (2) 'True'; and (3) 'False'. If you made a mistake it's probably because you allowed your opinions or existing knowledge to cloud your judgement. Thus it is well known that smoking increases your chances of having a heart attack, but the necessary information is not provided in the passage. In a similar way in Example 10 you have to be careful what you assume. The answer to (1) is 'No', because we have no information on non-venomous animals, and some may be dangerous. The answer to (2) is 'Yes', because according to the statements the animals which are venomous are dangerous to touch. Finally, the answer to (3) is 'No' again, because although we know there are animals which are safe to touch, we have no given information on which to base that conclusion.

Uses

Verbal reasoning tests are probably the most widely used type of ability measure. They are popular with employers because every job requires the ability to assess and use verbal information, whether it be understanding instruction manuals or writing management reports. In practice the formats illustrated by Examples 3 to 8 tend to be used in selection for semi-skilled, general administrative, clerical and customer service positions, whereas the verbal critical reasoning tests (Examples 9 and 10) are generally used for managerial and graduate selection.

The are many verbal tests on the market including *Working with Words, Verbal Comprehension, Verbal Usage, Verbal Reasoning, Verbal Analysis* and *Verbal Critical Reasoning* from Saville & Holdsworth Ltd. Other examples include the verbal component of the *Graduate and Managerial Assessment*, published by ASE; and the *Watson Glaser Critical Thinking Appraisal* from The Psychological Corporation.

Hints

A good way to prepare for verbal tests is to read and analyse complex verbal information. Try reading a quality newspaper and deciding if the assertions and assumptions made by the journalists are supported by the facts. You might also find it useful to read manuals and technical reports, and 'test' them for the logic of their arguments.

Other things to try are word games like Scrabble and the verbal logic puzzles you find in puzzle books available from newsagents. You must also attempt to expand your word power by reading more, and looking up any words you do not understand in a dictionary. A thesaurus, available from any good bookshop, will also be a useful addition to your library as it contains lists of synonyms and antonyms.

On a more technical note, when you are reading the questions in a verbal test it's worth remembering that if you read all the possible answers carefully, they will often give you clues as to the correct response. For example:

- the correct response is often shorter and more detailed;
- information given in the other answers may help to identify the correct response;
- the incorrect answers are often inconsistent or implausible;
- the use of absolutes (eg 'every', 'all') often appear in false statements.

Numerical Reasoning

Numerical reasoning tests measure your ability to understand and use numbers. They are concerned with the four basic arithmetic operations (addition, subtraction, multiplication and division), number sequences, simple mathematics and the use of numerical data to solve problems. The latter is usually the case with numerical critical reasoning tests in which blocks of information are provided that require both interpretation and the application of the appropriate logic.

Example 11: Arithmetic
Solve *without* a calculator.

(1) 24.7 x 4 = ?	(a) 84.3	(b) 89.8	(c) 92.3	(d) 96.7	(e) 98.8
(2) 719 + ? = 866	(a) 156	(b) 142	(c) 177	(d) 147	(e) 158
(3) ? – 48 = 112	(a) 152	(b) 162	(c) 154	(d) 160	(e) 149
(4) 25.6 ÷ 5.3 = ?	(a) 3.7	(b) 4.2	(c) 4.8	(d) 5.1	(e) 5.4

Example 12: Number Sequences
What is the next number in the sequence?

(1) 1	4	7	10	13	16	?
(2) 3	9	27	81	243	729	?
(3) 1	4	9	16	25	36	?
(4) 1	1	2	3	5	8	?

Example 13: Mathematics
Solve *without* a calculator.

(1) 25% of 500 = ?	(a) 120	(b) 250	(c) 125	(d) 220	(e) 175
(2) 3x + 12 = 18, x =	(a) 2	(b) 2.5	(c) 3	(d) 3.5	(e) 4
(3) (7 x 6) + ? = 70	(a) 38	(b) 32	(c) 18	(d) 42	(e) 28
(4) 1/6 as a decimal is	(a) 0.155	(b) 0.333	(c) 0.225	(d) 0.166	(e) 0.175

The answers to Example 11 are (e), (d), (d) and (c). Note that it's often a lot easier to work out the answer if you round the numbers, eg in question (1) if you look for the answer which is nearest to 25 x 4. In Example 12 the answer to (1) is 19, because the difference between each number and the preceding one is 3. Sequences like this, where you add or subtract a fixed number, are known as arithmetic progressions. In (2) the answer is 2187, because the next number is always found by multiplying the preceding number by 3. This is an example of a geometric progression. In (3) the answer is 49, because all the numbers are squares (1 x 1, 2 x 2, 3 x 3, 4 x 4, 5 x 5, 6 x 6, 7 x 7). In (4) the answer is 13, because the next number is the last two numbers added together. For the mathematically minded this is an example of what is known as the Fibonacci sequence. All these types of sequences are frequently used in numerical tests.

In Example 13 you need to go beyond simple arithmetic and understand how percentages work, simple algebra, the meaning of brackets and how to convert to decimal fractions. The answers are (c), (a), (e) and (d). All these mathematical operations are based on the sort of things you learn in secondary education.

Numerical critical reasoning tests present you with a range of numerical information, usually in the form of tables of data, charts or graphs. The task is to understand the meaning of the questions, find and interpret the appropriate data, and then perform the necessary calculations. In most cases the calculations are not difficult and the emphasis is on developing the correct problem-solving strategy. In this way, although the problems can seem complicated, they do not usually require a calculator. Indeed in most tests of this nature candidates are not allowed to use calculators.

Example 14: Numerical Critical Reasoning
Use the information below to answer the questions.

STUDENT EXAMINATION PERFORMANCE

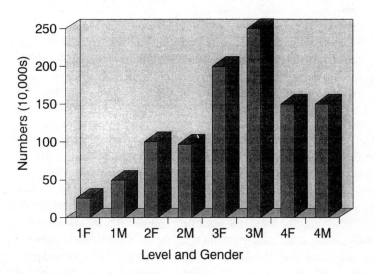

Qualifications by Level and Gender

College Qualifications by Level

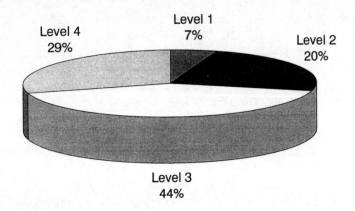

Level 1
7%

Level 4
29%

Level 2
20%

Level 3
44%

Key: Educational Levels are 1–4. Gender: M = Male and F = Female.

Questions:
1. How many women have Level 3 qualifications ?
(a) 250,000   (b) 200,000   (c) 2,000,000   (d) 2,500,000
2. What percentage of students have Level 2 or better qualifications ?
(a) 93%   (b) 83%   (c) 63%   (d) 73%
3. If the ratio of males to females with Level 4 qualifications is kept constant, but these qualifications make up 39% of the total, approximately how many more students will now have Level 4 qualifications ?
(a) 250,000   (b) 500,000   (c) 750,000   (d) 1,000,000

The Example 14 questions are quite typical of numerical critical reasoning tests as they involve the use of one or more charts and then a calculation. As you can see it is important to understand how the charts are labelled, in particular that the 'Qualifications by Level and Gender' chart has a scale marked in 10,000s. The answer to question (1) is obtained by reading off the value and multiplying it by 10,000, which gives (c). Question (2) relates to the pie chart with the answer being (a). Lastly, there are a number of ways of working out the answer to question (3), but if 29 per cent is equal to three million then 39 per cent must be equal to about four million. This gives a difference of one million, which is answer (d).

Uses

Numerical tests, especially those based on question formats like Examples 11 to 13, are used in selection whenever there is a need to assess numeracy or an aptitude for data manipulation. This covers many clerical and administrative jobs, as well as those in the banking and financial services sector. Graduates and managerial applicants can look forward to completing numerical critical reasoning tests with questions like those in Example 14.

As numerical reasoning tests are so commonly used there are many to choose from. In the UK the most popular include *Working with Numbers, Number Skills, Numerical Computation, Numerical Reasoning, Numerical Estimation, Interpreting Data, Numerical Analysis* and *Numerical Critical Reasoning*, all published by Saville & Holdsworth Limited. Other names to look out for are *Numerical Awareness* and *Numerical Estimation* (*Modern Occupational Skills Tests*), and the numerical component of the *Graduate and Managerial Assessment*, all published by ASE.

Hints

Make sure you are capable of performing simple calculations without a calculator. You can practise these when you go shopping by working out how much you will need to pay for your purchases, the real cost of discounted goods, the cost per minute of leaving your car in a carpark and so forth. It's also a good idea to practise with tables of information such as bus or train timetables, tables of currency exchange rates and the financial information contained in newspapers.

In terms of mathematical knowledge you will find it useful to understand:

- factors and multiples, eg powers and roots of numbers;
- fractions, ratios, proportions and percentages;
- different types of graphs, eg bar charts, pie charts and line graphs;
- simple statistics, eg how to work with frequencies or calculate an average.

If you are unsure about any of these aspects of mathematics consult a text book, especially any general text covering GCSE or equivalent level maths.

Perceptual Reasoning

Perceptual reasoning is about understanding and applying information presented in a diagrammatic form. Most tests of this nature are based on perceptual analogies, or involve the interpretation of diagrammatic rules. In both cases the answers can only be worked out by determining the visual logic of the information provided. Indeed they are deliberately designed so that a visual problem-solving strategy will work better than any other approach.

Example 15: Perceptual Analogies

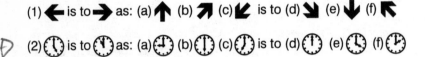

Example 16: Diagrammatic Interpretation
The following commands have the effects shown:

Command 1: ♥ ⇨ ▲	Command 4: ▼ ⇨ ♥
Command 2: ▲ ⇨ ▼	Command 5: ▲ ⇨ ■
Command 3: ■ ⇨ ♥	Command 6: ♥ ⇨ ▼

What will happen to the shape if the commands are applied?

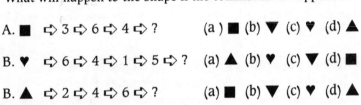

In Example 15, analogy (1) is a simple case of the different orientations of an arrow. The answer can only be worked out visually and is (a) and (e). In (2) you are presented with a series of clock faces, and the answer this time is (b) and (d). The quickest way to the solution is to realise that the difference between the two starting clocks is that the minute hand has rotated through 180 degrees, and to look for two other clock faces where this has happened. In Example 16 you are forced to imagine what will happen to a shape when it is transformed in various ways. Again this can only be done visually, and the answers are (c), (d) and (b).

Uses

Perceptual tests are often used to select for scientific, computing, engineering, design and technical craft positions. As with verbal and numerical tests they are also good predictors of performance in general managerial, administrative and office-based jobs. The same designs of tests are used with candidates applying for jobs at all levels. However the tests can be made more complicated by introducing additional variables, eg in Example 16 there could have been additional commands which changed the size of the shapes, the colour, or which only worked in combination with other commands.

A classic example of a perceptual reasoning test is the *Perceptual Test* (part of the *General Ability Tests*), published by The Morrisby Organisation. Others include the *Diagrammatic Reasoning* and *Diagrammatic Thinking* tests from Saville & Holdsworth Ltd.

Hints

The best form of practice for perceptual analogies is to buy a book which contains plenty of examples and to work out the relationships between the shapes or diagrams. You will discover that the relationships you find are similar to those used in abstract reasoning tests, and some verbal analogies. They will include changes in size, colour or orientation; and the membership of groups of shapes which get progressively more complicated, but which share similar features.

For tests based on diagrammatic interpretation, practise by producing your own diagrams which explain how a system works, eg draw a flow diagram which explains how to programme a video recorder. Any game which involves sequences of moves can also be good practice; this would include any board game based on strategy.

Spatial Reasoning

Spatial reasoning tests measure your ability to manipulate shapes in two dimensions, or to visualise solid objects presented as two-dimensional patterns. In the first case the test often presents you with a pattern which has some missing components, and you have to decide which of a number of alternate pieces will complete the pattern, or maybe just how many pieces are required. Other tests present two-dimensional objects which have been rotated or reflected, and you have to decide what has happened, eg whether or not a shape has been turned over. In those tests which require the visualisation of a solid object a number of patterns are presented which could be folded to make an object. Your job is to imagine which of the patterns would work in practice.

All spatial tests rely on you being able to imagine what would happen 'in your mind's eye'. This is something which many people find difficult to do, and some cannot do it at all. Thus, about 5 per cent of the adult population will find it impossible to imagine a two-dimensional shape moved through a third dimension. Psychologically speaking this is an interesting finding as it probably means that spatial ability is something which gets wired in to the brain quite early in life or, at the very least, by the end of the teenage years.

Example 17: Spatial Components

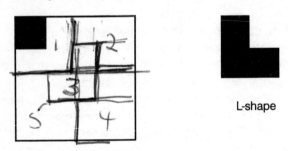

L-shape

How many of the L-shapes are required to fill the large square, without leaving any gaps ?

(a) 3   (b) 4   (c) 5   (d) 6   (e) Cannot be done

Example 18: Spatial Rotations and Reflections
All of the shapes below are the same, but they have been rotated into different positions. In addition *one* of them has been turned over, which one?

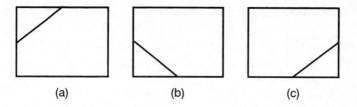

(a)   (b)   (c)

In Example 17 you will find that there is only one way of completing the square without leaving any gaps and this requires five
of the L-shaped pieces – answer (c). The solution is to fit one
piece around the black square in the top left-hand corner so that
you end up with a complete small square, and then to fit two further L-shapes on the corner of that square so that you complete a
diagonal going from the top left to bottom right. The remaining
gaps are both L-shaped, and require two further pieces. The best
way to work out the answer to Example 18 is to look for the one
shape which has been turned over like the page of a book.
Alternatively, you could look for two shapes, which when rotated
will sit exactly on top of each other, making the remaining shape
the one which has been turned over. Whichever strategy you use
you should get (b) as the answer.

The last example measures advanced spatial reasoning and
requires the ability to imagine patterns assembled into three-
dimensional objects. Questions like this can involve the visual
'assembly' and 'dis-assembly' of objects; objects which have been
rotated in space, or which are viewed from different angles (eg
from above, below, the side, the back); and objects which have different colours or markings on their surfaces. The last variety are
the hardest to deal with as they require an ability to imagine
shapes moved in three-dimensional space, *and* the ability to work
out the relative position of the markings on their surfaces.

Example 19: Spatial Assembly

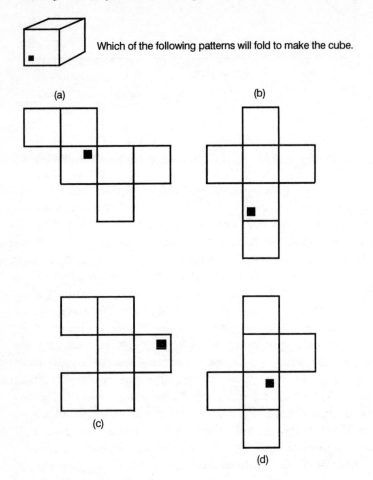

Which of the following patterns will fold to make the cube.

(a)

(b)

(c)

(d)

In order to answer Example 19 you first need to establish which of the patterns will fold to make the cube, and then which have the small black square in the correct position. If you look at the patterns carefully you will see that (a), (b) and (d) will all fold to make a cube. In this case they will also all produce the cube illustrated.

Uses

Spatial reasoning tests are used in selection for jobs where it is necessary to have a good eye for how things fit together, or to be able to cope with different shapes and patterns. This includes many practical jobs such as carpentry, decorating, floor-laying and sewing. Good spatial ability is also required in many production, technical and design activities where plans and drawings are used extensively. Thus, you would expect surveyors, architects, engineers and designers to have this sort of ability. It is also an ability which can be used in conjunction with modern 'visualisation' tools such as computer-aided design (CAD) packages.

Spatial reasoning tests are used less frequently than the other sorts of tests mentioned so far, but they do measure an ability which is a key component of many jobs. The tests on the market include the *Shapes Analysis Test*, published by The Test Agency; and the *Shapes Test*, from The Morrisby Organisation. Other frequently used examples are the *Spatial Reasoning* and *Spatial Recognition* tests from Saville & Holdsworth Ltd.

Hints

Spatial reasoning is a very practical sort of ability and so it is best practised by assembling and making things. For example, you could build models or assemble jigsaw puzzles. In fact these days there are three-dimensional puzzles which provide very good practice in imagining how complex parts fit together. If you are artistic you can also try drawing plans of objects from different angles, or try cutting out and assembling the sort of patterns illustrated in Example 19. Finally, if you have access to a computer drawing or CAD package you can draw objects which you can instruct the computer to move in three-dimensional space. This will allow you to see objects in any orientation and from any angle.

Mechanical Reasoning

Mechanical reasoning tests are designed to assess your knowledge of basic mechanical and physical principles. They usually contain questions which do not require any specialist knowledge, but which rely on you being able to work out what is happening. However, that's not to say that some knowledge of physics or mechanics, or practical everyday experience of simple machines and devices, would not be of help.

In virtually all mechanical reasoning tests you are presented with a question and a diagram. You have to determine what principle is being illustrated and select the correct answer from the options provided.

Example 20: Mechanical Reasoning

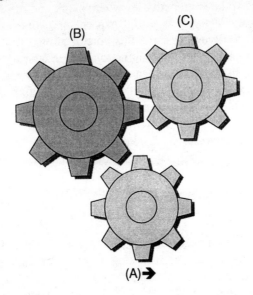

In which direction will C turn if A turns anti-clockwise?
(a) Clockwise (b) It will jam (c) Anti-clockwise
(d) Backwards and forwards

The answer to Example 20 is determined by imagining the effect of A on B, and then of B on C. In this way, even in this straightforward example, it involves step-by-step problem solving. If you approach the task in this way you will find that (c) is the correct answer. Looking at the other options, obviously (d) is incorrect, but so is (b). If you were tempted to answer (b) you were adding additional information to the diagram, eg by thinking that the cogs were too close together, or that friction would stop them turning. This is a common mistake with mechanical questions which can only be answered on the basis of the information provided, even if you think you know better!

Uses

Mechanical reasoning tests are used to assess people for practical jobs which require a working knowledge of mechanical principles. These are often positions which involve assembling components or running and maintaining machinery. As a consequence mechanical tests are often used to select mechanics, technicians and production workers.

One of the best-known mechanical reasoning tests is *Bennett's Mechanical Comprehension Test*, published by The Psychological Corporation. This was developed in the 1940s, and is still widely used throughout the world. Other more modern tests include the *Mechanical Test* from The Morrisby Organisation and *Mechanical Comprehension* from Saville & Holdsworth Ltd.

Hints

If you are interested in maintaining any form of machine, including a motor car, you are probably already practising this ability. Likewise, if you undertake 'do it yourself' projects, or repair things around the home, you are giving yourself scope to exercise your mechanical competence. Other things you can do are to work with construction kits (eg Technical Lego or Meccano); or to simply take household devices apart and put them back together again.

Research has shown that men are generally better at mechanical reasoning tests than women, so if you are female it's even more important that you understand the principles involved. However, whatever your gender, useful additional sources of information are GCSE level physics or technology text books. You will find that these give details on:

- **mechanisms**, eg balances, levers, linkages, gears, cranks and pulleys;
- **structures**, eg the effects of compression, stress and strain;
- **energy**, eg the transmission of heat, light and power;
- **forces**, eg gravity, and rotational effects such as centrifugal and centripetal force.

Other Ability Tests

The other main types of cognitive ability tests that you might encounter are concerned with checking detailed information. These are known as checking, data checking or classification tests. They are generally short in duration and present you with a number of tables of information which you have to check against each other. The function of this sort of test is to measure how quickly and accurately you can detect errors in data. This is an ability which is important in any job where detailed records are kept, eg banking, accounting, telephone sales and retailing.

Example 21: Data Checking

Look at the two tables of data below. Check each row and mark any differences you find between table A and table B.

Code	Table A Number	Band	Code	Table B Number	Band
127/34	2510	XA	127/34	2510	XA
128/35	2505	LM	128/53	2505	LM
129/36	2543	BA	129/36	2534	AB
218/43	3671	LM	218/43	3671	LM
218/44	3762	AB	218/44	3762	AB
219/45	3892	XA	219/54	3892	XA

In Example 21 there are differences in three of the rows. However, consider how much more difficult this test would be if there were 40 rows and 6 columns per table; and a mixture of numbers, letters, numbers and letters, and names and addresses – all to be checked in a matter of minutes.

Uses

As already mentioned, this sort of test is used to select people for clerical checking and data input jobs. Most of the major publishers produce tests which are a variation on the theme illustrated; with the *Speed and Accuracy Test* from the Morrisby Organisation and *Clerical Checking* from Saville & Holdsworth Ltd being good examples.

Hints

Data checking tests require an eye for detail and patience. One way to practise is to cross-reference codes and other details in catalogues and time-tables, or to check accounts or balance sheets. In short use any form of detailed information which you can check for its accuracy.

Manual dexterity tests

Finally, if you apply for jobs which require speed and accuracy with the hands you may be asked to take a manual dexterity test.

These are often in the form of peg boards where you are asked to place combinations of metal pins and washers in holes on a wooden board. Sometimes there are a series of tasks to complete in different ways, such as just using your left or right hand, both hands, or a pair of tweezers. More complex forms of dexterity test may require you to assemble a number of different types of components in a given time. These often look like construction kits, and involve the use of your hands and some tools. Commonly used dexterity tests include the *Peg Board* and *Fine Dexterity Tests,* both available from The Morrisby Organisation and the Test Agency.

Future Test Developments

In the short term you are likely to encounter more tests based on so-called business learning experiences. These are work simulation exercises in which you take the role of an employee in a fictional company or organisation. The tests work by teaching you what you need to know in order to complete a range of tasks, and then by finding out how good you are at applying your learning in practice. A typical scenario might be that you have just taken over a customer service desk, and your supervisor has briefly introduced you to the product and customer databases, and to a procedures manual. Your first customer arrives with a query...

Business learning exercises differ from traditional tests, which measure specific abilities, in that they present complete problem scenarios. In this way they present more realistic problems, and allow an employer to see more directly how you would perform in a real job. Arguably, these exercises are a fairer method of selection because they make no assumptions about your existing knowledge and, also, because they sample real job situations, they allow for a degree of self-selection. The last point is important because it saves time for employer and candidate alike.

Over the next few years more of these tests will be used, in particular for selecting potential middle and senior managers, and customer service and sales personnel. The pioneers in this area are Oxford Psychologists Press who publish tests such as the *Aptitude for Business Learning Exercises (ABLE).*

Looking further into the future you will find more computer-based tests which employ multi-media and virtual reality (VR) technology. For example, the next generation of personality questionnaires will allow you to explore work-based situations presented in the form of video clips with sound tracks. The task will be to select from a number of options how you would respond to the situation presented. It is likely that the way in which you respond to each situation will then determine what happens next – just like real life! In a similar way the questions presented in ability tests will be modified according to the answers you give. It will also be possible to monitor how you go about solving a problem. Ultimately this means that psychologists and employers will be able to learn about your style of problem solving, and this will become more important than whether or not you get the answer correct.

Other developments include the use of VR to put you 'inside' a test. Thus, by wearing the appropriate equipment it will be possible to place you in a world of tests in which you can 'see' and 'feel' the questions. This may sound like science fiction but a number of systems do already exist, and VR-based exercises are already used for selection and training by the US Airforce and the British Royal Navy.

The pace of technological change is such that within the next 10 to 20 years it is reasonable to suppose that a combination of new test designs, VR and the WorldWide Web will allow any person anywhere in the world to be assessed using a realistic simulation of any job.

Ten More Ways to Improve your Performance

The details and hints given for each type of ability test will help you to prepare for most forms of testing. The key points listed at the end of Chapter 2 also provide important guidance on how to prepare for a test session. However, as you will see, there are a number of additional tips which can also help.

Tip 1: keep going!

As I have suggested elsewhere the best policy is to try and complete as many questions as you can in the time allowed. However, you will find that different tests have different time limits. For example, here are the timing ranges for the tests covered in this chapter:

- Abstract Reasoning   30–40 minutes
- Verbal Reasoning   15–20 minutes
- Verbal Critical Reasoning   30–40 minutes
- Numerical Reasoning   15–20 minutes
- Numerical Critical Reasoning   30–40 minutes
- Perceptual Reasoning   15–20 minutes
- Spatial Reasoning   10–20 minutes
- Mechanical Reasoning   15–20 minutes
- Data Checking   8–10 minutes
- Manual Dexterity   5–8 minutes

Clearly, while it's good advice not to waste time on questions which you find difficult, you have more scope in some tests than in others to go back to a question you have not answered. As a rule of thumb if a test is under about ten minutes long it's better just to answer as many questions as you can, and not to return to those you may have left out.

Tip 2: double-check your answers

It is often suggested that when you attempt to answer the questions in a test that your first impressions are usually correct. This implies that if you have the time it is better to try and answer any questions you have left out, rather than change any of your existing answers. Interestingly, research has shown this to be an incorrect assumption; with one US study indicating that you may be three times as likely to change a wrong answer to a right one, than to make a right answer wrong. This suggests that any time you spend double-checking is time well spent.

Tip 3: guess with intelligence

If you do not know the answer to a question, should you guess? The two things to consider are how you're going to guess, and whether or not the test is negatively scored. When tests are negatively scored you have marks deducted for incorrect answers. This may or may not be announced at the beginning of the test, but if the instructions say that you should not guess then it is actually better to leave questions out. Conversely, if the instructions suggest that you should not leave any questions out, then it is probably safe to guess.

On the subject of how to guess, it is better to guess the answers to questions about which you have some knowledge. For example, if there are five options and you can completely eliminate two of them, you have a one-third chance of hitting the right answer. These are obviously better odds than a pure guess which would give you a one-in-five chance of picking the correct response. However, you should bear in mind that if you are forced to guess a lot of the answers, even if you can reduce each to a one-in-three chance, then you are unlikely to score a very high mark. The reason is that your chance of correctly guessing the first question is one-in-three, and of the second question is one-in-three, but of correctly guessing both of them your chance is one-in-nine (one-third *times* one-third). The more you guess, the worse are the overall odds. Even so, informed guesswork is much better than randomly picking the answers.

Tip 4: read the questions twice

Many people work out the correct answer to a problem and then fill in the answer sheet incorrectly. A common mistake is to mix up the answer choices. Consider the following example:

> ### Example 22: Verbal Sequences
> What is the next word but one in the following sequence?
> Century...   Decade...   Year...   Month...?
> (a) Hour   (b) Minute   (c) Day   (d) Week   (e) Second

It's easy to look at a question like this and to decide correctly that (c) is the right answer, but to mark (d) instead. That's because you have confused 'd' with the first letter of 'day'. Another thing that people do is to misread the question, in this case not to notice that the question asks for *the next word but one*. This would mean that while you fully understood the sequence you would answer (d) again, which of course is incorrect. The moral of the story is always to pay very close attention to the questions, otherwise you will lose marks even when you actually know the correct answers.

Tip 5: estimate your answers

In most numerical tests the questions are usually designed so that you do not have to work out the answers exactly in order to choose the correct responses. This would imply that it is better to work out rough answers and check them against the options, rather than spend time calculating things precisely.

Tip 6: don't be afraid of numbers

An ability to deal with numbers is a key requirement in many jobs. If you don't like mathematics the *only* way you are going to improve is to face your fear head on. Go to a library or a bookshop, find a maths book you understand, and work through some examples.

Tip 7: watch out for distracters

When test questions are written the designer will include different types of answer choices. Naturally one of these will be the correct answer, but the others will be distinct sorts of incorrect answers. Here are some examples:

- If the correct answer is '67.5' a number of 'distracters' will be included such as '6.75', 675 and 6750. The estimation approach suggested in Tip 5 should help you to avoid picking any of these by accident.
- Body is to food as engine is to: (a) spark (b) wheels (c) fuel (d) exhaust.
  The correct answer is (c), but it's surrounded by distracters, all of which are related to the word 'engine'.

The trick with distracters is to realise that they are there in the first place, and not to be seduced by things like near misses, or word associations.

Tip 8: think about the question order

It makes sense to answer the questions you find the easiest first. This means that it is not always advisable to answer the questions in the order presented. However, if you do adopt this tactic make sure you do not get out of sequence on the answer sheet. Also, if you read the questions as you go along you will find that your unconscious mind has a chance to work on them, and sometimes you will find it much easier to get the answer when you return for a second time.

Tip 9: use all your time allowance

Even if you are finding a test hard going, use all the time you are allowed, and work right up to the last second. If you finish early double and triple check your answers.

Tip 10: practise, practise, practise!

Sometimes a few more marks will make all the difference. It pays to put as much energy as you can into preparing yourself for psychometric tests.

Key Points

- There are about 50 different abilities that can be measured, but most assessments are based on combinations of only 6 types of test.
- The most frequently used tests measure abstract, verbal, numerical, perceptual, spatial and mechanical reasoning.
- Other types of test measure psychomotor abilities like hand–eye co-ordination; physical abilities like static strength (the ability to use continuous muscle force to lift, push and carry – important in jobs like fire-fighting); and sensory abilities, such as correct colour vision (important for designers, electricians, chemists and pilots).
- Each type of ability test has characteristic types of questions. Extensive details have been given in this chapter.
- There are exercises you can do to prepare for any test which is based on knowledge or experience (attainment tests). You can also improve your performance on other types of tests by following the hints provided.
- Preparation is the key to test success. No employer will expect you to be an authority on tests, or test taking, but intelligent preparation in the weeks before a test session will help to give you an edge over the other candidates.
- In those cases where employers use cut-off scores (see Chapter 1), a few extra marks can make the difference between success and failure. Ensure that you do not make avoidable mistakes.
- There are many sources of valuable information and practice material, such as text books, quiz books and books containing example questions. These can all be bought in large bookshops, or are available from libraries.

Chapter 4

Personality Questionnaires

Personality, like ability, is a key influence on how a person performs at work. It's particularly important in all those situations which involve interaction and co-operation with other people; namely all managerial, supervisory, customer oriented, team or group based activities.

Personality is usually measured by using a self-report questionnaire. This is a 'test' that directly asks *you* about aspects of your own personality; allowing for a consistent and objective measure of things like how you cope with pressure, your preferred way of dealing with other people and your general behavioural style. In this way personality is really the characteristic way in which you respond to situations; or your preferred way of behaving in particular circumstances, or towards other people.

It has recently been estimated that there are 1200 self-report questionnaires on the UK market alone, and that they are used by over 50 per cent of medium to large-sized organisations. Their popularity is no doubt due to the speedy and objective way in which they can give a detailed picture of what a person is like, and the ease with which this 'profile' can be matched against the *behavioural* requirements of a job. However, whatever the use, it's important that the aspect of personality that is measured is genuinely part of you, rather than merely the consequence of a particular situation; and also something which allows predictions to be made across a range of different activities. For example, knowing that you are an extrovert, but that you behave in completely different ways in different social situations, wouldn't be of much use.

Another critical thing about personality is that it does not change dramatically over time. This does not mean that it never changes, rather that it's stable enough to be measured in a meaningful way. Again, it wouldn't be very useful to ask you to complete a questionnaire one day, only to get a completely different result if you did the same questionnaire a week later. This is obviously rather important from an employer's point of view as employment is a long-term business. As such it's valuable to know how you are likely to behave over the months and years you will be with a particular organisation, not just on the day you happen to have been tested.

To summarise, personality questionnaires are a standard and objective way of discovering your preferred ways of behaving and relating to other people. They allow an employer to see if you fit the behavioural requirements of a particular job; or, conversely, if you're already in a job, to identify your training and development needs. From a purely selfish point of view they also allow you to 'choose' work which better suits you temperamentally, and which you will find more interesting and satisfying.

Different Personality Questionnaires

There are many different designs of personality questionnaire, but the vast majority fall in to only one of two psychological camps. These are those which assign you to a specific personality *type*, and those which are based on a *trait* approach – a trait being an aspect of personality which you possess to a lesser or greater extent.

Type questionnaires

There are a number of commonly used personality questionnaires which are based on a type approach, yet they all owe their basic structure to the work of the Swiss psychologist Carl Jung. He developed a theory to describe the *predictable* differences between the ways in which people behave in different situations. The crux of his argument was that the variations in our behaviour are caused by the way we prefer to use our minds. The use of the word 'prefer' is important here because the Jungian approach is rooted in an either/or way of looking at personality, ie: you take this approach *or* that approach, not a bit of both.

In terms of preference the two options we have when our minds are active are to receive information (perceiving), or to process it and come to a decision (judging). Moreover, if the focus is on perceiving, then there are only two ways of taking on board information, sensing and intuition; likewise judging splits into thinking and feeling. Thus, there are four key processes which we use to understand the world around us, the only further modification being our orientation towards the world, either extroverted or introverted. The former shows a concern for social interaction with other people, and a desire to understand and experience the world at large. The latter shows a fascination for the 'inner world' of thinking, feeling and reflecting.

To summarise, the type approach allows your personality preferences to be expressed on 4 double-ended scales, giving a total of 16 main types. However, that's not to say that you're 'stuck' with one of 16 particular ways of behaving, rather that you have a natural and comfortable way of behaving. An analogy that is often used is that of having to write with your 'wrong' hand. If you do this it feels unnatural and clumsy, and requires concentration, whereas if you use your preferred hand your writing is automatic and you don't have to think about it. In the same way we all have a definite preference, say, for perceiving or judging; and if we are able to use our preferred approach we are generally more confident *and* competent.

This method of personality classification does not imply that there are 'good' or 'bad' personalities. Thus 'extrovert' does not equal 'good with other people', or 'introvert' 'shy' and 'retiring'. People simply differ in their approaches and, if you happen to have a similar approach to another person, you will tend to share similar sorts of behaviours and attitudes. These may be more or less useful, strengths or limitations, depending on what you are trying to do. The other thing to realise is that type can be independent of ability, in that the sort of 'intelligence' you have does not dictate the sort of person you are.

The type approach is mostly used in an intra-personal sense, that is for development and exploration of the self. It can also be used to select people for jobs, but usually only if the questionnaire is designed so that direct comparisons can be made between people in terms of the *amounts* of particular characteristics they possess (a normative approach – see Chapter 1). This being said questionnaires based on the type system are completed by millions of people every year. In consequence it makes sense to spend a little more time exploring the 'preferences' in more detail.

Extroversion – introversion

Extroverted people are concerned with the world which surrounds them. They like to interact with other people, and are fond of talking and debating. In social situations they tend to take the initiative, and to search out other people. However, sometimes their enthusiasm leads them to say things without thinking, and they may inadvertently hurt others. In a work context extroverts are active and people oriented; and do not like, for example, slow, repetitive jobs.

Those who are introverted tend to be more involved in their own private world. They like to analyse what they are going to say before they say it, and may prefer to communicate in writing. There is a 'self-contained' air to their dealings with other people, and they may sometimes be regarded as being a little too cool and detached. At work introverts need quiet so that they can concentrate (they don't like open-plan offices), and are quite happy to work alone.

Judging – perceiving

Those who prefer a judging style live in a structured and orderly way. They like to have plans and schedules, and work to a timetable. Their whole life is organised, controlled, and executed in a precise manner. In the workplace they need order and a plan of action, and work best when they can organise their time thoroughly. They also like to follow a task through to an obvious and tangible conclusion.

In contrast the perceiving person reacts in a flexible and spontaneous manner, and adapts to what is going on rather than attempting to control it. This casual approach often manifests itself in last-minute planning and an 'open-ended' approach to life. Unlike the judging person, the perceiver feels positively claustrophobic if things are planned to the last detail. At work this can cause problems, especially with jobs which need to be completed within tight time deadlines. However, many perceiving people would claim that they produce their best work at the eleventh hour!

Sensing – intuition

This aspect of personality is concerned with how you prefer to receive information, with sensing people concentrating on the information which flows from their senses of sight, hearing, taste, touch and smell. Such people are usually practically oriented and assess things in a step-by-step way. They tend to trust what they sense, and are rooted in the 'here and now'. In the work context this manifests itself in a preference for dealing with facts, and sensing people can usually be relied upon to be right about matters of detail.

The intuitive person has a more abstract approach and is interested in the inter-connections between things, not necessarily the things themselves. The concern is more with the 'big picture' and how information fits together in different patterns. Indeed, the truly intuitive person may be particularly good at developing new insights and working out different ways of doing things. From a work point of view this means that intuitive types tend to follow their noses, and may actually overlook certain facts. There is also a tendency to work in short, inspirational bursts, rather than make steady, continuous progress.

Thinking – feeling

A preference for thinking indicates a detached and logical approach to problem solving. The style is characterised by the search for cause and effect, and a reduction of situations to their component parts. There is little room for fancy, and such an analytic and impersonal style is perhaps best described as 'scientific' (and for fans of the TV programme *Star Trek* is perhaps most akin to the Vulcan objectivity of Mr Spock). At work the thinker is firm minded and principled, but may tend to overlook the human side of things.

In stark contrast the feeling person bases decisions on their likely impact on other people. The mentality is one of identifying with the thoughts and feelings of others, and of adopting the most sympathetic approach. This is sometimes described as 'tender-mindedness', as the aim of any action is to take the most compassionate line. Thus, feeling individuals are distinguished by their understanding and supportive style, and are usually driven by a strong sense of the value of the individual. In a work scenario this translates into a desire to please other people, and to ensure a harmonious working environment.

Questionnaire formats

The questions in a personality questionnaire can be presented in a number of different ways. A format that is often used in type questionnaires is one which forces you to choose between two options, or to rank a number of statements in terms of how true they are of you.

> ### *Example 1: Forced Choice*
> Do you prefer to:
> (a) plan what you do in advance; or
> (b) react to things as they happen?

If you answered (b) to the above question you would be saying that you like to wait and see what happens rather than organise yourself before events. That's because the two parts of the question score on different personality scales. However, the big problem with this approach is that you have not been able to indicate how true you believe *either* of the statements to be. In reality you may be neither very organised nor very reactive; indeed you may be a combination of both depending on the circumstances. What this means is that tests constructed in this way can only broadly comment on you as an individual; and they cannot (unless used very judiciously) be applied to selection situations. The following example should make this point even clearer.

> ### *Example 2: Ranking*
> Rank in order of interest, 1 to 3, the following sports:
> Golf   [ ]
> Football   [ ]
> Tennis   [ ]

Suppose we both answered *Example 2*; we might both order the sports (1) Tennis, (2) Golf, (3) Football. However, in practice, you might be a professional tennis player and a keen golfer, and I might just enjoy watching them all on the television. So what this sort of approach cannot do is to show the strength and application of a particular interest or, in the personality sense, the different amounts of a particular characteristic. This is a very important consideration for employers who are interested in the relative balance of characteristics between potential employees.

How are type questionnaires used?

Type questionnaires are widely used in organisations for development and training purposes. They can help to show the sort of environments in which people prefer to work, the way in which they are likely to go about their work, and the ideal personality of any colleagues with whom they would work best. This last concern has become more important in recent years with the increase in work teams, groups or cells. Indeed, the team approach is now common in most areas of employment from manufacturing plants, such as those producing cars and aircraft, to retail businesses like banks, supermarkets and shops.

By far the most widely used type questionnaire is the *Myers-Briggs Type Indicator® (MBTI®)*, with over 3.5 million people taking it throughout the world each year. It is published by Consulting Psychologists Press Inc in the USA, and is also available from Oxford Psychologists Press in the UK. Other type questionnaires include the *Jung Type Indicator*, published by Psytech International Ltd, and the *Occupational Type Profile* produced by Selby Millsmith Ltd.

Trait questionnaires

Trait questionnaires are concerned with the differing amounts of personality characteristics which all people possess. So these questionnaires are designed to measure how much of a certain trait you possess, eg how extroverted you are compared to another candidate for a job, or how stable you are compared to people in general. The traits that are measured are assumed to influence the ways in which we behave, and are so predictive of behaviour. Indeed, those who design questionnaires which measure traits, such as the famous American psychologist Raymond Cattell, have defined personality as 'that which permits a prediction of what a person will do in a given situation'. However, before we move on to look at the different sorts of traits that can be measured, it is useful to think about the difference between a trait and a state. This isn't just of academic interest as it's important that a questionnaire is measuring a stable and enduring aspect of a person's personality, rather than just the current state of that person. After all, we pass through different mental states during the day, with our mood changes depending on the situations in which we find ourselves. Naturally, most questionnaires attempt to concentrate on the measurement of traits, but there are some that assess both trait and state. Thus, whether or not you are an anxious person can be measured, alongside an indication of whether or not you were anxious at the time you completed the questionnaire.

There are about 20,000 words in the English language which label traits. Obviously many of these relate to the same underlying traits, but even so that still leaves a considerable range of different characteristics. As such it should come as no surprise that questionnaires have been designed that measure anything from 3 to 30 or more aspects of personality. This may sound confusing but not all questionnaires are attempting to measure every part of someone's personality, and many are actually concentrating on what are recognised as the five key dimensions of personality. These are known as the 'Big Five', or the 'Five Factor Model', and are reckoned to be the primary personality dimensions which underpin all observable behaviour! I should say, however, that there isn't universal agreement on this question and many psychologists would argue that there are as few as three main dimensions. This being said, the 'Big Five' are worth exploring in some detail. Incidentally, along the way you will notice that there are some similarities with the type descriptions given in the last section, demonstrating that both type and trait approaches are covering more or less the same ground.

The big five

A great deal of research points to the fact that personality can be broken down into five main dimensions or domains. These concern how people approach situations and tasks (action); the style of their reasoning (thinking); how they behave towards other people (relating); the underlying nature of their emotions (feeling); and how they regulate their actions (conformity).

Action

This concerns an individual's attitude towards other people in a work or personal context. In many questionnaires it is either referred to as 'tough-mindedness' or as 'agreeableness'. The tough-minded person being someone who is primarily results orientated, and who may disregard other people's feelings in pursuit of a particular goal. Those who are very tough-minded have little time or patience for those who need support, and tend to work best with other like-minded colleagues.

It is, of course, possible to possess the complementary personality characteristics and be a tender-minded person. This suggests a warmer, more people-focused individual who has a genuine concern for the feelings of other people. This sort of person is also more likely to achieve results by listening to different viewpoints, and to adopt a co-operative, trusting and consensual style. In this way those wishing to discuss sensitive and personal issues are far more likely to approach this sort of person than their tough-minded, results-driven counterpart.

Thinking

This is about the structure and organisation a person brings to a situation. It also relates to self-discipline and, characteristically, to attention to detail. The 'structured' person places great value on order and control. This manifests itself in a very tidy and systematic way of approaching tasks. For example, projects are often planned to the last detail, and organised in a precise and meticulous manner. Thus a highly structured person leaves nothing to chance, and is always conscious of what to do and how long it will take. In extreme cases this can appear somewhat obsessional (especially to a 'low structure' individual), or overly perfectionist.

A 'low structure' person tends to have a more relaxed and casual approach to life. As long as jobs are completed such people do not worry about formal structures or schedules. They are not particularly concerned with personal organisation and, as such, can sometimes appear somewhat disorganised. In many cases they may miss important details or, because they are less ordered, be late for appointments or meetings. In a managerial sense they have a greater preference for the over-view or the strategic approach; rather than the detail or tactical level of a project.

Relating

Classically this refers to how a person relates to other people in the environment. It is the personality dimension that is most used by the lay-person when describing other people as it concerns extroversion and introversion.

The extroverted individual is sociable, outgoing and attracted to other people. Such a person is energetic and enthusiastic, and is prepared to voice an opinion and to become involved in most things. At work, people-centred and high-profile roles have the most appeal, especially those which rely on the skills of negotiation and persuasion. However, extroverts can be rather impulsive and sometimes take risks without properly weighing up the odds. They can at times also appear rather domineering, and find it difficult to believe that others do not share the same enthusiasms they do.

The introverted character is less concerned with other people and tends to be more introspective. In general there is a less excitable and more moderate outlook, and a tendency to take a more cautious and restrained approach to work. Introverts are also far less likely to want to be 'in charge' or to seek the limelight. In many ways the attitude is one of personal challenge (the inner game), rather than an open competition with other people. In terms of analogy it's like wishing to break a personal best time in athletics, rather than race against other people.

Feeling

This relates to the level of confidence you have as an individual. It is sometimes also referred to as neuroticism, anxiety or emotionality. However, basically it concerns how self-assured you are as a person.

Those with high self-confidence tend to be relaxed and optimistic. They enjoy responsibility and like to be put to the test. When they are put under pressure they react in a calm and organised way, and have faith in their own ability to cope. At work they are able to deal with unexpected events with ease, and put their views forward with confidence and conviction. Other people are likely to see them as being highly personally competent and assertive.

Those with low confidence, or high emotionality, have difficulty coping with stress and pressure. While they *can* take on responsibility, they may find it places a considerable emotional strain on them. They also tend to question their abilities, and are generally more pessimistic and cautious than those who are confident. In the work sense they prefer predictability and tend to shy away from complex, open-ended situations. This suggests that routine jobs in large, supportive organisations are likely to suit them the best.

Conformity

This refers to a person's need for variety, or the way in which an individual responds to change. It is also sometimes called creativity, independence or openness to experience.

The conforming person works within existing rules and regulations, and usually deals with problems using well-established methods. The approach is measured and conservative, and can be described as being 'by the book'. Such individuals are also practically minded and more comfortable with implementing plans rather than creating them. The conforming person is happy operating within the status quo and does not have a burning ambition to be seen as creative.

In contrast the non-conforming person is concerned with individual expression. This frequently indicates an unconventional and creative thinker, who actually resents structure and order. Thus non-conforming people actively seek out and enjoy discovering new ways of doing things, and like to have variety in their work. At work the non-conformer is seen as being innovative and change oriented. There is a resistance to the traditional way of doing things, and a preference for risk taking. The latter can sometimes prove dangerous for an organisation as uncontrolled risk taking can lead to business failure. However, modern management thinkers do suggest that some non-conforming people are desirable in an organisation as they provide the catalyst for change or, as it is sometimes described, the grit in the oyster. This is a useful expression as it's the grit that ultimately leads to the pearl.

Trait questions

There are two main ways in which the questions in trait questionnaires are arranged. These involve either rating a list of statements, or indicating choices between a number of statements.

Example 3: Rating
Mark the [1] if you strongly agree with the statement; the [2] if you agree; the [3] if you are unsure; the [4] if you disagree; and the [5] if you strongly disagree.

1. I enjoy social gatherings   [1] [2] [3] [4] [5]
2. I am always late for appointments [1] [2] [3] [4] [5]
3. I avoid taking risks   [1] [2] [3] [4] [5]
4. I like playing team games   [1] [2] [3] [4] [5]

Note: Sometimes the questions appear in the form of lists of adjectives (creative, dominant, tense, active, social, sensitive etc), rather than statements. In this case all you do is indicate your level of agreement, 1–5, with a series of words.

Example 4: Two from four choice

For each block of four statements indicate which one is most like you [M], and which one is least like you [L]. Leave the other two statements blank.

I am ...

1. A highly organised person	[M]	[L]
Anxious when meeting new people	[M]	[L]
The 'life and soul' of the party	[M]	[L]
An energetic person	[M]	[L]
2. Even tempered	[M]	[L]
Skilled at practical problems	[M]	[L] etc

Example 5: One from two choice

For each statement indicate whether you think it is true [T] or false [F]:

1. I like to try new ways of doing things	[T]	[F]
2. I find it difficult to relax after a hard day's work	[T]	[F]
3. I am an optimistic person	[T]	[F]
4. I enjoy organising meetings and gatherings	[T]	[F]

Example 6: One from three choice

For each statement indicate whether you think the statement is true [T]; false [F]; or if you are not sure [?]:

1. People should sort out their own problems	[T]	[?]	[F]
2. I can get more done when I can work alone	[T]	[?]	[F]
3. I like telling people funny stories	[T]	[?]	[F]
4. I show my emotions easily	[T]	[?]	[F]

All the above are common ways of presenting questions and, as you can see, some allow more choice than others. In particular one of the biggest differences is between those questionnaires which allow you to respond 'unsure' [?], and those which force your choice between a number of options. You may feel that you don't want to be forced to answer one way or the other; however questionnaires are designed like this to stop you being indifferent to everything. That's because if you were unsure, or couldn't make your mind up about most of the statements in a questionnaire, it would be impossible to produce an accurate picture of your personality.

How are trait questionnaires used ?

Trait questionnaires are used for selection and development purposes. Unlike type questionnaires they can be used to select people for jobs because they allow an employer directly to compare one person with another. Therefore it is possible to say that person A is more extroverted than person B, and also how much more extroverted A is than B.

Questionnaires of this design are used in most of the large companies in the UK and the USA. Variations are also available in most European and Asian countries, translated into the appropriate languages. Virtually all measure the 'Big Five' personality dimensions, although in practice they usually do this by breaking the five principle components down into a number of sub-scales. So, for example, in the UK, the most popular questionnaires contain 16 and 30 scales respectively.

The names to look out for are the *Sixteen Personality Factor Questionnaire™ (16PF)*, published by ASE in the UK and IPAT in the USA. Also the *Occupational Personality Questionnaire®️ (OPQ®️)*, published by Saville & Holdsworth Ltd, and the *California Psychological Inventory™ (CPI™)*, published by the Consulting Psychologists Press Inc, and distributed by Oxford Psychologists Press. Other questionnaires you might come across are the *Rapid Personality Questionnaire (RPQ), Manchester Personality Questionnaire (MPQ), Personal Profile Analysis (PPA)*, and the *NEO Five Factor Inventory™ (NEO-FF™)*. The first two were designed in the UK, while the others have their antecedents in the USA but are also widely used in the UK.

How to Complete a Personality Questionnaire

At present most personality questionnaires come in the form of a question book and a separate answer sheet. Thus your task is simply to read the questions and complete the answer sheet using a pencil. However, many questionnaires are becoming available on computer and so you may find yourself using a keyboard to respond to questions presented on a computer screen. There are also a number of other less common variations (see Chapter 2), but irrespective of how the questions are physically presented they will always be in one of the formats described previously. In addition it's worth remembering that if you are tested by computer you will not be expected to be a keyboard expert (it's your personality that is being assessed, not your typing skills); and you will always have the opportunity to practise and to ask questions before the assessment begins.

There follows some general guidelines on how to approach any personality questionnaire:

- **Be as honest as you can**. The best advice is to give the best, most straightforward answer to any question. Do not look for trick questions or be tempted to give the answers you feel will do you the most good, but which are untrue. The reasons are that it is difficult to 'bend the truth' consistently when you may be answering up to 200 questions; and you may also inadvertently emphasise one aspect of your personality at the expense of another. Likewise you do not know the ideal profile for a particular job, and you may actually distort your personality results in the wrong direction.

  In addition, many questionnaires contain special scales which are designed to detect those who are presenting themselves in an overly positive light. These are called 'impression management' or 'motivational distortion' scales, and contain questions which check how honest and consistent you are being. For example:

I have never been late for an appointment	True	False
I have never told a 'white lie'	True	False

  Some questionnaires also contain scales which can help to identify potential criminal behaviour, or addictive personalities. Clearly such information can be of value to employers in the retail and financial sectors, although it should be stressed that no questionnaire can produce a fool-proof indication of such behaviour. This being the case they are always backed up by other sources of information, eg personal references.

- **Think about a typical day**. The questions you will be asked relate to how you usually behave at work. If you don't have a job just think about how you deal with other people in social situations, or how you deal with situations at school, college, or wherever you spend your time.

- **Trust your first impressions**. Although most questionnaires have no time limit, it is better to answer the questions quickly rather than agonise over each one. The reason is that in this case, unlike ability tests, your first thoughts are usually the most accurate. It's also a good idea to work quickly because it will often take you between 30 and 40 minutes to finish a questionnaire even when you are trusting your first impressions. That's not to say that every questionnaire will take this long, as some are quite short, and will only take about ten minutes to finish. The latter are often used to recruit people for customer service or sales positions.

- **Read the questions carefully.** If you study the questions it is often possible to determine which broad aspects of personality are being measured. For example, extroversion or *relating* questions frequently refer to sociability, risk-taking, impulsiveness, lack of responsibility and high levels of emotional energy. In contrast introversion questions often cover the opposite characteristics such as a dislike for social occasions and more thoughtful decision making.

  In a similar vein tough-mindedness or *action* questions often concern achievement orientation, competitiveness, assertiveness, manipulation and a lack of sympathy for other people, whereas tender-mindedness questions focus on a feeling, trusting and co-operative style, or on an empathic way of behaving.

  Likewise questions concerning anxiety or *feeling* will be based on issues such as low self-esteem, obsessive behaviour (such as repeatedly checking things or always having to be early for appointments) and a lack of personal autonomy. The contrasting confidence questions will concern things like being able to respond in crises, being able to take criticism, not worrying over mistakes, and generally taking a relaxed view of life.

  The thinking or *structure* questions will relate to how organised a person is in everyday life. So high-structure questions will tap behaviours such as ordering and controlling people and things; also anything relating to detailed planning and organising tasks in advance. The low-structure items will then cover a dislike for organisation and planning, and especially things like a poor sense of time or lack of personal discipline.

  Finally, *conformity* questions will concern practicality, conservatism, tried-and-tested methods and conscientiousness. Their low-conformity counterparts will cover creative and divergent thinking, a frustration with rules and regulations, a need to be able to express individuality, and a search for variety and mental stimulation.

In describing the content of questions like this, the argument is that if you understand what the questions are asking, you will be able to give better and more genuine responses.

- **Answer all the questions.** It's important that you answer all the questions or it will not be possible to get a valid picture of your personality. Also, don't get stuck on questions you don't feel are relevant, but just give the best and most immediate answer you can. A related problem is 'arguing' with the questions, ie over-analysing the questions to such an extent that you don't know what is being asked. Unfortunately, some questions will appear rather ambiguous, but as before the most profitable thing to do is just to give your first reaction.

- **Know yourself.** The more self-knowledge you have the easier it will be to present an accurate picture. Remember that personality questionnaires are really only asking you to report on yourself, and so it makes sense to be as aware as you can of your own personality. You can do this by consulting self-test books (look in a good bookshop); or by asking other people to describe how they see you. In fact one of the most interesting things you can do is to write down, say, ten adjectives which you feel sum up your personality, and then get someone who knows you well to do the same thing. If you then compare the two lists you may get a few surprises!

- **Know the job.** Just as it's useful to know something about your personality before you complete a questionnaire, it's also beneficial to know about the job for which you are applying. What sort of a person are they looking for? You will get some clues from the job advertisement and also any other literature you can study before the assessment session. For example, you may find that an advert refers to particular 'competencies' (see Appendix 1 for more details), or that a company publishes a house magazine or newsletter. Do these give a feel for the ideal employee? What impression do you get of the organisation? Perhaps it's large and traditional, and favours 'middle-of-the-road', detail conscious and stable workers. Or is it small, fast moving and creative? Does this suggest more dynamic, risk-taking and extroverted individuals?

Finally, always follow the directions printed in the front of the questionnaire booklet, and pay particular attention to any instructions given by the test administrator. It should also be a comfort to remember that personality questionnaires are designed to assess you in a fair and objective way, and to help you choose the work to which you are most suited. Clearly there's little point in fulfilling all the requirements of a job in terms of ability and experience, only to find that you cannot cope with the people aspects of a particular position.

Other Self-Report Questionnaires

There are a number of other aspects of human temperament that can be measured apart from personality. These include qualities such as values, motivation, integrity and interests. All of these additional factors are assessed at one time or another, and the next section deals with each in more detail.

Values

These are the 'personal concepts' that we hold which determine how we deal with everyday life. They are the standards or principles which guide our behaviour towards other people. In practice, of course, it's difficult to differentiate between values and aspects of personality; but, unlike personality, values are influenced more by the culture in which we live.

Values questionnaires are often used to complement personality assessments, and are usually focused on how you cope with everyday problems and/or your relationships with other people.

The questionnaires are generally designed in a forced-choice format (see Example 1: Forced Choice) and measure values such as:

- honesty;
- self-respect;
- equality;
- goal orientation;
- self-control;
- independence;
- altruism;
- social support.

Values questionnaires are often used in assessment programmes for middle and senior managers. The best-known example is probably the *Global Gordon's Personal Profile Inventory (Global GPP-I)* distributed by ASE.

Motivation

Motivation is closely related to the issue of values and is one of the most important things to assess during the selection process. However, it's also one of the hardest to measure as we all claim to be highly motivated when we apply for jobs; in particular we are likely to put on a great show of interest during the interview.

In practice motivation can be defined as the energy which we are likely to bring to bear on work tasks. This is useful for an employer to know as it is essential to select people who are genuinely motivated, and committed to making a success of a job. It's also important to know what a person wishes to strive towards, and those activities or circumstances which both increase *and* decrease motivation.

Motivation questionnaires are often used with managerial, professional and supervisory staff, and aim to identify the range of factors which energise and support individual behaviour. For example, people are often motivated by some of the following:

- high work load and tight time deadlines (**pressure**);
- responsibility and authority (**power**);
- exceeding personal goals and targets (**achievement**);
- working as part of a close-knit team (**affiliation**);
- competing against other people (**competition**);
- self-development and personal learning (**growth**);
- praise and recognition from other people (**recognition**);
- earning a good salary (**reward**);
- having a stable and dependable job (**security**);
- working in a well-organised business (**structure**);
- working for a well-respected organisation (**prestige**);
- being able to maintain high personal values (**ethics**);
- having a good position (**status**);
- being able to move up an organisation (**progression**);
- having control over work activities (**autonomy**);
- the desire to succeed (**achievement**);
- the work ethic, or work itself (**drive**);
- creative and varied work activities (**interest**);

You may have noticed that some of these motivational factors are the same as the values mentioned previously. This goes to show that it is actually quite difficult to untangle values from motivation, and that in all probability they interact with each other. So, if you're the sort of person who places great value on independence you may well be motivated by having control over what you do **(autonomy)**, and being able to develop your personal competence and extend your repertoire of skills **(growth)**.

Employers find that motivation questionnaires are a good way of comparing job applicants or current employees against job demands; and also against the management style of an organisation. The latter is of increasing importance as many businesses are starting to pay attention to their organisational 'culture'. For example, if you have a strong need for structure, clear paths of progression and security, you might find it difficult to work for a small organisation with little in the way of hierarchy or long-term promotion prospects.

An example of a motivation questionnaire is *Motive-A*, published by the Test Agency. Another popular questionnaire is the *Motivation Questionnaire (MQ)* distributed by Saville & Holdsworth Ltd.

Integrity

Integrity is the weasel word used by psychologists when they are talking about honesty; and so integrity tests are designed to discover if you are likely to be an honest and reliable employee. At present most of these come from the USA and are the result of the adverse publicity generated by polygraph tests. If you are unfamiliar with the polygraph approach it is a lie detector test which is based on the fact that the electrical resistance of your skin varies when you are telling a lie. This is measured by placing a series of electrical pads on your fingers or hands. It is clearly a rather worrying way of assessing honesty, and also a method which is unacceptable in a selection context.

In consequence, modern integrity tests are questionnaire based and are designed to indicate those aspects of a person's potential work behaviour which may give cause for concern. In many integrity tests the questions relate to how you would respond to a variety of common situations involving money, 'time-theft' and tardiness; and your attitude towards rule breaking and criminality in others. Here are some examples:

- If you found £50 in the street would you hand it in at a police station?
- Would you take a day off 'ill' if you felt you had been over-worked?
- If you received too much change in a shop would you give it back?
- Do you know anybody who steals regularly?

These are fairly obvious questions, but even so they can be quite instructive in showing someone's potential (dis)honesty. Interestingly, there are differences between the sexes in the replies which people give, and also between different countries. Thus recent research by a major firm of UK test publishers has shown that women are far more likely to return excess change in a shop; and that, culturally, of all the European nations, the Spanish are the least likely to give money back. Needless to say these sorts of variations have to be taken into account when applying integrity tests.

Integrity tests are used by retail organisations and other businesses which rely on personal honesty, eg, the police, security services, financial organisations and airlines. An example of an integrity test is *Giotto* published by the Psychological Corporation.

Interests

Interest questionnaires are constructed so that they indicate your workplace preferences, or those activities which you feel you would enjoy. Thus the two main types of interest questionnaires that you will encounter are those which assess management interests; and the more general variety, which measure general occupational interests.

Management interest questionnaires focus on the balance of management functions which are of interest. For example, you will find yourself indicating your level of interest in areas of management such as:

- Production and Manufacturing;
- Technical Support and Services;
- Research and Development;
- Transport and Distribution;
- Sales and Marketing;
- Personnel and Training;

- Finance and Accounts;
- Administration and Control;
- Legal and Management Services;
- IT and Computer Systems.

In addition some questionnaires compare your interest in, say, producing accounts and managing the finances of a business, with the amount of experience you have of doing such a job. This allows an employer to compare your interest, or enthusiasm for something, with your actual experience.

Management questionnaires can also measure your interest in distinct work activities, especially those relating to the day-to-day control of a business. For example:

- written communication;
- oral communication;
- decision making;
- problem solving;
- developing and training;
- negotiating and persuading;
- predicting and forecasting;
- information collection and analysis;
- organising people and resources.

Such questionnaires are routinely used to assess existing or future managers. However, as with measures of values, they are usually used alongside other sources of information such as personality questionnaires and ability tests.

An example of a management interest questionnaire is the *Management Interest Inventory (MII)*, published by Saville & Holdsworth Ltd.

General occupational interest questionnaires are often used with school leavers, graduates and others to assess interests over the entire range of work activities. One of the best-known systems is that produced by the American psychologist, John Holland, who developed a way of breaking down people's work interests into six main types: Realistic, Investigative, Artistic, Social, Enterprising and Conventional.

- **Realistic** people prefer activities in which they can use practical ways of solving problems. They value concrete things and prefer tangible rewards for their endeavours such as money or status. Realistic people can be described as being genuine, hard-headed, practical and persistent.

- **Investigative** people prefer activities which involve a systematic and analytic way of working. They also like tasks which involve an observational and scientific approach. Investigative people can be described as being critical, rational, intellectual and curious.
- **Artistic** people place value on individual expression and enjoy language, art, music, drama and writing-based activities. They can be described as being aesthetic, cultural, emotional, intuitive and imaginative.
- **Social** people prefer activities which allow them to influence other people, and to be involved in helping, caring, managing, training, developing and informing. The emphasis is on interpersonal skills, and so social people can be described as being persuasive, understanding, empathic and co-operative.
- **Enterprising** people are concerned with making things happen, and the manipulation of other people and resources to achieve personal success. They often perceive themselves as being aggressive and as possessing leadership abilities. The enterprising person can also be described as being ambitious, energetic, self-confident and adventurous.
- **Conventional** people prefer activities which involve the detailed and systematic use of information. They like to organise and use data in a precise and disciplined way. They can be described as being conforming, conscientious, methodical and thrifty.

Naturally it is possible to be a mixture of the above types and to have more than one area of interest. Indeed this is true of most people, although some combinations are less likely than others, eg conventional and artistic do not often go together, whereas enterprising and social do.

When this system is used in careers guidance the questionnaire yields a three-letter code which indicates your area of interest, eg SEI. This is then used to check against a dictionary of occupational codes which contains well over 12,000 different jobs – from abrasive grinder and hassock maker, to uptwister tender and yeast washer. By the way, in the example given, SEI is the code for an occupational psychologist.

An example of an interests questionnaire based on the work of John Holland is the *Self-Directed Search (SDS)* which is distributed by the Morrisby Organisation, and published by Psychological Assessment Resources Inc in the US. Other interest questionnaires include *Passport* and the *Rothwell-Miller Interest Blank,* both distributed by The Morrisby Organisation, and the *General* and *Advanced Occupational Interest Inventories (GOII; AOII),* published by Saville & Holdsworth Ltd.

Finally...

In this chapter the intention has been to introduce you to the idea of personality and the various ways in which it can be measured. Some of you may believe that reducing personality to four or five dimensions is a gross over-simplification. However, before coming to such a conclusion consider the following analogy used in the marketing of a leading US personality questionnaire:

...there are only three primary colours and yet they allow us to produce every single colour, tone and hue in the world...

In a similar way the Big Five personality dimensions allow us to describe the complete spectrum of personality, because when each dimension is broken down into its component scales there are literally millions of different combinations.

Key Points

- There are about 1200 different personality and other self-report questionnaires available to psychologists and employers.
- Type questionnaires place you in a fixed personality category, and are used for development and training purposes.
- Trait questionnaires measure how much of a personality factor you possess. They are used for selection and assessment as they allow you to be directly compared with other people.
- Research has indicated that there are five main dimensions of personality. These cover action, thinking, feeling, relating and conforming.
- There are six main types of questions in personality questionnaires. These include those which force your choice, and those which allow you to rate or rank a series of statements.
- There are a range of strategies which will help you complete any personality questionnaire. These involve being honest (and

not second guessing the questionnaire designer); placing your answers in the appropriate context; trusting your first impressions; reading the questions properly; and knowing yourself and the job to which you are applying.

- Some questionnaires contain scales to detect whether you are bending the truth. While there is nothing wrong with presenting yourself in the most positive way it is very difficult to disguise your real self. The best advice is just to be as honest and straightforward as you can.

- There are many other types of questionnaires apart from those that directly measure personality. For example, questionnaires which assess personal values, integrity, motivation and interests are also common.

- In order to present a strong and consistent picture of your personality you must be positive, open-minded and truthful in your answering. Remember that personality questionnaires are designed to help you find the right job; getting a position on the grounds of inaccurate results is only likely to lead to low performance, and ultimately a great deal of stress.

Chapter 5

The Inner Game

The preceding chapters have concentrated on the mechanics of psychometric testing, such as what tests measure and the practical steps you can take to improve your performance. Advice was also provided on what to do if you suffer from examination nerves or are anxious at the thought of being tested. This chapter develops these final points further and concentrates on the management of the 'inner game' – those things which you can do to achieve a positive frame of mind in advance of any test session. Such preparation is just as important as being familiar with the things you may be asked or, for example, knowing when it is wise to guess the answers to questions.

What sort of attitude do you have ?

Think about the prospect of being tested and look at the two lists of words below. Which list best describes how you feel ?

- Enthusiastic
- Excited
- Relaxed
- Positive
- Confident
- Optimistic
- Motivated
- Reassured

- Anxious
- Tired
- Defensive
- Despondent
- Apprehensive
- Pessimistic
- Alarmed
- Threatened.

If most of your thoughts are centred on the right-hand list you need to explore techniques for becoming more positive about the testing process. Even if you were only drawn to just two or three of the right-hand words, you would still benefit from considering some of the techniques which follow.

Becoming motivated

Test success is all about getting yourself motivated for the task in hand. This in turn hinges on whether you have a positive or negative attitude to the testing process. Hopefully, if you have read the rest of this book you should be feeling much better prepared for future assessments already. However, in a more general way, the difference your overall mental attitude can have on your chances of success should also be taken seriously. The reason is that tests bring out our fears; they make us confront aspects of our character which are closely linked to our sense of self and ego. They often make us think about the 'negative' things which may be revealed about our abilities and personality. In fact many of us have developed a sort of active pessimism. We believe that if we allow ourselves to be tested the truth will be discovered and we will be exposed as being less intelligent than we thought we were, or to have a less than perfect personality. Worse still, somebody else will know. Interestingly, these thoughts only seem to multiply as we accumulate more academic qualifications and honours. This is not least, of course, because we feel we have more to lose if our test results do not live up to our previous performance.

The first thing to do is to stop these thoughts dead in their tracks. Why are we pessimistic about our potential performance when most of the time things do work out? Why have we allowed ourselves to be blinded by the few things that go wrong, and not cheered by the many things that go right every single day? The truth is that negativity breeds negativity, and if you're not careful you will find that your imagined fears continually block your progress. A case in point are the estimated 40 per cent of job applicants who do not attend test sessions when invited. They have allowed their fear of the unknown to stop them at the very first hurdle. Incidentally, if you think of this from a positive perspective, it means that just by making an appearance at a test session the odds have already narrowed in your favour.

The trick to achieving a positive frame of mind is to switch your thinking from the apprehensive and reactive, to the energetic and proactive. This means building a new self-image based on accepting the challenge of life, rather than adopting the (easier) 'Why make an effort because it's all going to go wrong?' attitude. Not only that, researchers have demonstrated that those with a positive outlook on life, who believe that they can make a difference, actually live longer! So there's at least one other very good reason for adopting a new way of thinking about yourself.

Changing your outlook

Most of us are very hard on ourselves. We feel that we haven't achieved what we would like, and that we don't live up to other people's expectations. To add to our woes we also like to blame ourselves when things don't work out, and continually to kick ourselves for our imagined inadequacies and personal failings. This you might say is the human condition; but it doesn't have to be so. Why not try being kind to yourself? This may sound like an amazingly obvious thing to do, but do you do it? The answer is probably no, because in our society we tend to choose self-punishment over reward. As a result we never reinforce our own positive behaviour because we are too busy feeling guilt, or blame, or that we could have done better.

To break these self-defeating thoughts you need to:

- stop blaming yourself and
- acknowledge your success.

At a practical level this means avoiding the tendency to personalise problems. In real life this is one of the biggest differences between positive and negative thinkers; as the latter are always accepting responsibility for negative events and turning them into feelings of failure. Positive thinkers do not take this view and concentrate on the learning experience. As most counselling psychologists would agree, this involves moving away from the event itself, to placing a positive construction on the way in which we experience and think about what has happened. In terms of technique this involves making the most of your 'mistakes', and then forgetting them.

Concentrate on thinking about what you have learnt from an experience, not whether or not it was a success or a failure.

Another key technique is to stop applying double standards. This relies on a realisation that you are probably just as competent as anybody else; or, to put it another way, are you undervaluing yourself simply because you are you? Is it just that you have a higher standard for yourself than you do for other people? Many of us fall into this trap at one time or another as the standards we set for ourselves are not fixed. Thus, when we are at the point of succeeding, we unconsciously move the 'goal posts' further back. In this way we are never really satisfied with what we have achieved, and always feel that we could have done better.

Give yourself permission to have confidence in what you know and who you are.

When you have succeeded in achieving a particular goal, whatever that might be, give yourself credit and allow yourself to acknowledge your success. This involves mentally 'patting yourself on the back' and telling other people what you have done. Many people do not do this because they believe it is being arrogant, boasting or 'blowing their own trumpet'. In truth, as long as you do not overdo it, it is a mechanism for confirming to yourself that you have succeeded.

You might also find it useful to use self-affirmations. These are phrases which you can repeat to yourself which will help you boost your self-confidence. The most famous being that devised by Emile Coué: 'Every day, in every way, I am getting better and better' (readers may recognise these words as having been used by Inspector Clouseau's boss, Dreyfus, in the *Pink Panther* films). Such verbalisations are actually good ways of changing your frame of mind. Thus, each morning, set aside some quiet time and affirm how confident you feel in yourself. You don't have to use Coué's words, just choose some which are meaningful to you. At the beginning you will probably think that nothing is happening, but if you persevere you will get results. That's because you are teaching yourself something new: *how* to feel positive.

Take credit for your successes and affirm your belief in yourself.

Another fundamental difference between positive and negative thinkers is the amount of effort each puts into a task. Negative thinkers frequently work on the 'if at first you don't succeed, give up' principle. This is a shame because confidence actually comes from doing things, and seeing a job through to the end. For example, you may be the sort of person who finds some aspects of mathematics difficult to understand and, in consequence, have never actually applied yourself to understanding any of it. When asked how you feel about maths you probably say that you are 'no good', and that you have never passed any examinations. Indeed some people actually take a sort of pride in their lack of ability. What you're actually doing is justifying your lack of performance by your lack of application! It really only serves to underline the fact that you weren't prepared to invest enough energy in the learning process. That's because it's always easier not to try and so have no chance of achieving something (no expectations and no disappointment), rather than try your best to master something with the chance that you could succeed or fail (high expectations and possible disappointment). The first route leads nowhere; the second allows for the possibility of personal development. To put it another way, there are no guarantees, certainly not when it comes to trying to land a good job; but if you don't put everything you have into the venture your chances of success are severely limited. The only thing you can do is to keep going in the belief that you will succeed; and if you do believe in yourself, you will.

Accept the challenge and give it everything you have got ...

Finally, as I've mentioned a number of times in this book, remember that psychometric tests are designed to identify the best person for the job. So, just as it's not in an employer's interests to give a position to someone with the wrong balance of skills, abilities, experience and personality; it is not in an applicant's interests to be offered a position which is entirely unsuitable. This implies that even if you're not successful the self-knowledge you will gain will help you in future applications. However, if you study the 'form' and understand the requirements of the job *and* the selection process you will stand a much better chance of getting the job you want. Good job hunting!

Some Final Brain Teasers

If you enjoy mental problems, try the ten which follow. The answers are given on pages 115–17.

Question 1

What is the next letter in the sequence?
O ... T ... T ... F ... F ... S ... ?
(a) S (b) T (c) O (d) F (e) Impossible to tell

Question 2

Evil is to Doom as Live is to: (a) Breathe (b) Happy (c) Mood (d) Expire (e) Feeling

Question 3

Add three lines to make four squares:

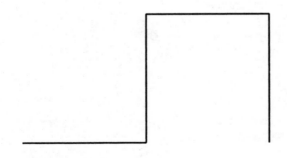

Question 4

Without using a calculator. If you divide £10 by one-quarter and give your answer in pence, how many pence will that be ?
(a) 250 (b) 400 (c) 2500 (d) 4000

Question 5

The famous mathematician, Euler, was once asked to solve the following problem:

In the town of Konigsberg there are seven bridges across the river Pregel. The bridges link two islands to each other, and also to the banks of the river. Is it possible to go for a non-stop walk, crossing all seven bridges only once ?

The Konigsberg Bridges

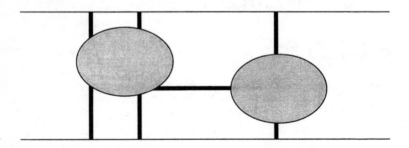

Question 6

What is the missing number?
17 ... 13 ... 11 ... ? ... 5 ... 3 ... 2
(a) 9 (b) 7 (c) 6 (d) 8 (e) 10

Question 7

If BACON = 35, what does EGGS = ?
(a) 28 (b) 32 (c) 35 (d) 38 (e) 41

Question 8

Now try your hand at a well-known reasoning problem developed by the psychologist Peter Wason.

Look at the four cards below. Each card has a letter on one side and a number on the other. Which cards need to be turned over in order to decide whether the following statement is true or false ?

'If a card has a vowel on one side it will have an even number on the other side.'

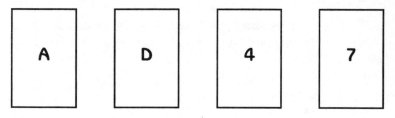

(a) D and 4 (b) A and 7 (c) D and 7 (d) A and 4 (e) A and D

Question 9

Look at the square of letters below. What are the missing letters?

AC	KM	MO
GI	IK	CE
QS	OQ	?

(a) CK (b) QM (c) EG (d) AG (e) IS

Question 10

What are the next *two* symbols in the sequence?

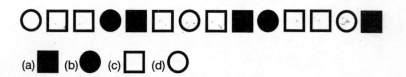

Appendix 1

Competencies

The word 'competency' is widely used in business and personnel psychology, and refers to the behaviours which are necessary to achieve the objectives of an organisation. A competency is also something you can measure; and lists of competencies form a common language for describing how people perform in different situations.

Every job can be described in terms of key competencies. This means that they can be used for all forms of assessment, including appraisals, training needs analysis and selection. In fact it is in the selection context, especially in advertisements, that you are most likely to come across competencies. For example, the following were recently used in a recruitment campaign for a major UK car retailer:

'You will have good **interpersonal** and **communication skills**, and have substantial personal **impact**. Also familiar with IT systems, you will enjoy **problem solving**, and make the best use of your **analytic skills** ... This is a job which requires an **innovative** approach, coupled with a commitment to **teamwork**. You will be **quality focused**, and committed to building on our enviable reputation in the industry.'

This is quite a typical list containing eight different competencies. It is these sorts of competencies that personnel professionals aim to detect by examining your application details, and through assessment processes such as psychometric testing and interviewing.

Different Competencies

The competencies which follow are all commonly used in job specifications, and form the criteria against which to assess people. I have described each one and indicated if it can be assessed using a psychometric test or questionnaire. You can use this list, in conjunction with job advertisements, to decide which aspects of your ability or personality may be assessed by the tests you are asked to complete. Surveys have shown that the most popular competencies asked for are communication, leadership, judgement, initiative, motivation, analytic skills, planning, innovation, interpersonal skills and numeracy.

Individual competencies – your personal attributes

- **Flexibility**   This is the ability to change direction, or modify the way in which you do something. It includes a willingness to try, adaptability and a positive outlook.
  Measurement: Personality or Motivation Questionnaire.
- **Decisiveness**   This is a readiness to act and to take decisions. It involves making a balanced judgement and taking the appropriate actions.
  Measurement: Personality Questionnaire.
- **Tenacity**   This is the ability to persevere and stick with a problem until it is solved. It is also marked by the ability to abandon a problem if it is unsolvable.
  Measurement: Personality Questionnaire.
- **Independence**   This is a willingness to question the accepted way of doing things; also the strength of mind to pursue a course of action based on your own convictions.
  Measurement: Personality or Values Questionnaire.
- **Risk Taking**   The extent to which you are prepared to take calculated risks. An important factor in many jobs including sales and manufacturing.
  Measurement: Personality or Values Questionnaire.
- **Personal Integrity**   The maintenance of high personal standards; also the implementation of appropriate ethical and moral norms in a work context.
  Measurement: Personality, Integrity or Values Questionnaire.

Interpersonal competencies - dealing with other people:

- **Communication**   The ability to convey information clearly and accurately, both orally and in writing; also includes a recognition of the importance of actively listening to others.
  Measurement: Verbal Reasoning Test (for written communication).

- **Impact**   The skill of creating an immediate and positive first impression on other people. A vital ability for many managerial and selling positions.
  Measurement: Personality Questionnaire.
- **Persuasiveness**   The ability to persuade and influence others to your point of view. This also involves being seen as believable and authoritative.
  Measurement: Personality Questionnaire or Specialist Sales Personality Questionnaire (if appropriate).
- **Personal Awareness**   This is being aware of other people and the environment in which they operate. It means taking into account other people's thoughts and feelings before acting.
  Measurement: Personality Questionnaire.
- **Teamwork**   This means contributing in an active and co-operative way with other team members. It includes supporting other people, and making decisions by consensus.
  Measurement: Personality Questionnaire or Team Role Indicator.
- **Openness**   This is being able to encourage different points of view without becoming defensive; also the ability to build on the contributions from other people.
  Measurement: Personality Questionnaire.

Analytical competencies – the elements of decision making:

- **Innovation**   The ability to come up with imaginative and practical solutions to business problems.
  Measurement: Personality or Creativity Questionnaire or specialist Ability Test.
- **Analytic Skills**   The ability to break a situation down in to its component parts, recognise what needs to be done and plan a suitable course of action in a step-by-step way.
  Measurement: Critical Reasoning Test.
- **Numerical Problem Solving**   The ability to understand and analyse numerical information. This includes financial data and statistics presented in reports, tables, graphs, charts etc.
  Measurement: Numerical Reasoning Test.
- **Problem Solving**   The ability to evaluate a situation and to identify an appropriate solution which meets the customers' needs – the skill of 'turning a problem in to a solution'.
  Measurement: Critical Reasoning Test.

- **Practical Learning** This involves being able to absorb and learn new methods, and then applying them to job-related activities.
  Measurement: Specialist Ability Test or Learning Styles Questionnaire.
- **Detail Consciousness** The ability to process large amounts of complex information. This includes all forms of written, verbal and visual data.
  Measurement: Ability Test or Personality Questionnaire.

Managerial competencies - taking charge of other people

- **Leadership** This is being able to take the role of a leader and guiding the actions of other people accordingly. The focus is on achieving results by working through other people.
  Measurement: Personality Questionnaire or Leadership Style Questionnaire.
- **Empowerment** This is the concern for developing other people, and giving them the authority and responsibility to act on their own volition.
  Measurement: Specialist Personality Questionnaire or Values Questionnaire.
- **Strategic Planning** This is the ability to maintain a broad overview ('helicopter' view) of business activities which allows you to plan for the future.
  Measurement: Personality Questionnaire or specialist Ability Test.
- **Corporate Sensitivity** This is the demonstration of an understanding of where a business is going, and of its agreed goals and strategies.
  Measurement: Personality or Interests Questionnaire.
- **Project Management** The ability to define the requirements of a project and to lead a group of people towards a specified goal.
  Measurement: Specialist Personality Questionnaire or Team Role Indicator.
- **Management Control** The appreciation that businesses need to be controlled and that the work of subordinates needs to be organised.
  Measurement: Specialist Personality Questionnaire or Management Interests Indicator.

Motivational competencies – the things that drive you

- **Resilience**   The ability to 'bounce back' in the face of adversity or when things do not go according to plan.
  Measurement: Personality Questionnaire.
- **Energy**   The personal store of energy which you bring to work and which helps you maintain a high level of performance – your 'stamina' or 'drive'.
  Measurement: Personality Questionnaire or Motivation Questionnaire.
- **Motivation**   This is the ability to motivate yourself *and* those around you. It's also related to knowing when to take control of a situation, and when to issue orders to other people.
  Measurement: Personality or Motivation Questionnaire.
- **Achievement Orientation**   This is the drive to achieve results, and to set targets which provide personal challenges.
  Measurement: Personality, Values or Motivation Questionnaire.
- **Initiative**   This is the ability to work in a proactive way to anticipate events, and to act on opportunities as they arise.
  Measurement: Personality Questionnaire.
- **Quality Focus**   This is the commitment to getting a job done well, and to recognising that the quality of a product or service is of critical importance.
  Measurement: Specialist Personality or Values Questionnaire.

The preceding list is by no means exhaustive but it should give you an idea of the sort of competencies required by employers. You should also recognise that some of these competencies are difficult to measure with psychometric tests alone (especially those which I have indicated as needing 'specialist' measures), and many are assessed using a combination of methods, eg tests, interviews and group exercises involving a number of candidates.

Group Exercises

Group exercises are designed to assess your problem-solving abilities, and responses to other people, in typical work situations. In some ways they are similar to the business learning exercises described in Chapter 3, but they involve a combination of both interpersonal and analytical skills. The following example will give you an idea of what is involved.

The runway exercise

'You are a member of a group of four planning officers who have to decide on the location of a new runway for a major regional airport. You have at your disposal a range of maps, plans, costings, economic surveys and the results of a local planning inquiry.

The task is to decide which one of three options best balances the demands of the regional economy, the local population and the environment. The group has two-and-a-half hours to produce an argued recommendation.'

This sort of exercise typically produces a range of arguments both for and against all the options. For example, in this case some of the key issues include the following:

Option 1: Easy access to motorway and rail systems
Strong support from regional businesses
Enthusiastic backing from local Member of Parliament
but...
Most expensive (£2.5 million)
Will destroy habitat of rare bird species
Requires some compulsory land purchase

Option 2: Least expensive (£1.8 million)
Uses some existing derelict land
Preserves habitat for rare birds
but...
May produce a slight noise problem
Location makes it most difficult to build
Opposition from local pressure groups

Option 3: Costs £2 million (£3 million minus £1 million grant aid)
Requires no compulsory land purchase
Has room for business park (creating 2500 new jobs)
but...
Is opposed by national conservation groups
Requires a 'green-field' site
May create a long-term pollution problem.

Which option would you choose ?

If you are ever faced with one of these exercises the most important thing to remember is that there isn't one perfect solution. What the assessors are looking for are reasoned and logical arguments which take into account all the information provided. It's also important that all members of the group agree on the solution, and consequently that decisions are made on a consensual basis. Should you require further information on group exercises the best place to look is in books which include chapters on Assessment Centres, eg *Interviews Made Easy*, published by Kogan Page.

Appendix 2

Codes of Conduct

When you attend a psychometric test session the employer is morally obliged to ensure that you are treated in a fair and reasonable manner. In most cases the test session will follow the guidelines laid down by an appropriate professional organisation, or commission, eg:

- American Psychological Association (APA)
- British Psychological Society (BPS)
- Commission for Racial Equality (CRE)
- Equal Opportunities Commission (EOC)
- Institute of Personnel and Development (IPD).

The guidelines produced by these bodies include advice to employers on appropriate training for test users; the factors to consider before using tests; how to choose ability tests and personality questionnaires; the scoring and interpretation of tests; and the importance of monitoring and evaluating test use. While there is no legislation in the UK directly governing test use, employers are reminded that if tests indirectly discriminate against certain groups they may come under the provisions of the Sex Discrimination, Race Relations, Fair Employment and Disability Discrimination Acts.

There are similar provisions in other countries and, indeed, some, like the USA, operate stringent controls over all forms of psychological assessment.

At a practical level you can expect the employer, or the organisation that delivers psychometric assessments, to adhere to guidelines covering the following points.

- **Test invitation** You should be informed at least seven to ten days in advance if you are to attend a test session.

- **Practice tests**   If appropriate the testing organisation should provide you with practice test materials.
- **Special arrangements**   You should be allowed to make adequate arrangements to be able to take tests. This may involve confirming wheelchair access, that you will be able to hear the test instructions, and so on.
- **Ethics**   You should be aware before the test session of the types of test you will be asked to complete, and what they measure. Ideally the employer should explain how the tests relate to the requirements of the job, ie why they are relevant.
- **Administration**   The test administrator should ensure that tests are administered according to the instructions provided by the publisher. The test room should be at a reasonable temperature with adequate lighting. It should contain comfortable seating, and be free from noise or other distractions.
- **Confidentiality**   Your test results should be kept confidential and secure. In the UK if information is held on computer you must be informed of your rights under the Data Protection Act.
- **Access**   Knowledge of your results should be restricted to those who need to know; and results must only be interpreted by those who are appropriately trained.
- **Feedback**   You should be informed before the test session of whether or not you will receive feedback on your results. However, while you have no 'right' to your test results, most enlightened companies will give you some feedback on your performance.

Appendix 3

Test Publishers

Major UK publishers:

Most publishers produce extensive catalogues and an increasing number also distribute information on the WorldWide Web.

Assessment for Selection and Employment (ASE)
Darville House
2 Oxford Road East
Windsor
Berkshire
SL4 1DF
Telephone: 01753 850333

Hodder & Stoughton
338 Euston Road
London
NW1 3BH
Telephone: 0171 873 6000

The Morrisby Organisation (TMO)
(formerly Educational & Industrial Test Services Ltd)
83 High Street
Hemel Hempstead
Hertfordshire
HP1 3AH
Telephone: 01442 215521
Website: http: //www.morrisby.co.uk

Oxford Psychologists Press Ltd (OPP)
Lambourne House
311-321 Banbury Road
Oxford
OX2 7JH
Telephone: 01865 510203
Website: http: //www.opp.co.uk

The Psychological Corporation Ltd
24–28 Oval Road
London
NW1 7DX
Telephone: 0171 267 4466

Psytech International Ltd
The Grange
Church Road
Pullox Hill
Bedfordshire
MK45 5HE
Telephone: 01525 720003

Saville & Holdsworth Ltd (SHL®)
3 AC Court
High Street
Thames Ditton
Surrey
KT7 0SR
Telephone: 0181 398 4170
website: http: //www.shlgroup.com

Selby-Millsmith Ltd
30 Circus Mews
Bath
BA1 2PW
Telephone: 01225 446655

The Test Agency Ltd
Cray House
Woodlands Road
Henley-on-Thames
Oxfordshire
RG9 4AE
Telephone: 01491 413413

Some US publishers

Many UK companies still use tests which are direct imports from the US. The main publishers include the following:

Consulting Psychologists Press, Inc
577 College Avenue
PO Box 60070
Palo Alto
California
94306

CTB / McGraw-Hill
Del Monte Research Park
2500 Garden Road
Monterey
California
93940

Institute for Personality and Ability Testing, Inc (IPAT)
1801 Woodfield Drive
Savoy
Illinois
61874

Psychological Assessment Resources, Inc (PAR)
PO Box 98
Odessa
Florida
33556

Science Research Associates (SRA)
155 North Wacker Drive
Chicago
Illinois
60606

Answers: Some Final Brain Teasers

Question 1

The letters are the first letters of the numbers: One, Two, Three, Four, Five and Six. The next letter is 'S' for Seven, and so the answer is (a).

Question 2

'Evil' is 'Live' spelt backwards. Therefore you need to look for a word which is 'Doom' spelt backwards. The word is 'Mood', and so the answer is (c).

Question 3

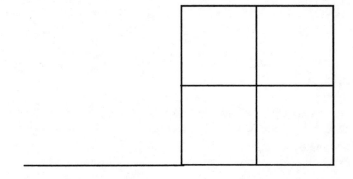

The key to this problem is to read the instructions carefully. It does not say that you have to use all the existing lines, or that the lines you add should not cross.

Question 4

£10 is 1000p. If you divide 1000 by 0.25 you get 4000. The answer is (d).

Question 5

It is not possible to go for a non-stop walk crossing all the bridges only once. Sometimes the answer is 'No' ! (If you are intrigued by this problem you might be interested to look in a book on graph theory. A 'graph' being a set of points which are joined by a number of lines – like the bridge problem. Consult a mathematics text book under the heading 'network' or 'Euler's formula'.)

Question 6

All the numbers are only divisible by themselves or one. This is a series of descending *prime* numbers and therefore the missing number is 7. The answer is (b).

Question 7

This question uses the position of the letters in the alphabet, so A=1, B=2, C=3, D=4, E=5 etc. In this way if BACON = 35 (which is 2+1+3+15+14), then EGGS = 38. The answer is (d).

Question 8

In order to decide if the statement is true or false you need to turn over 'A' and '7'. This is answer (b). If you think the answer is (d), look at the question again!

Question 9

The square is composed of two sets of leap-frogging letters. One set starts with 'A' and 'C'; the other with 'C' and 'E'. If you write out the alphabet and mark off the pairs of letters you will see what is happening. The missing pair are 'E' and 'G', and so the answer is (c).

Question 10

A deceptively simple question, but one which can be quite confusing. The circles are alternating white and black, but what about the squares? In fact the correct answer is (c) and (b).

I hope you enjoyed the questions.

Further Information

There are a range of books available for those who would like to explore psychological testing in more depth. Among the many titles to be found in libraries and bookshops, the following may be of interest:

Using Psychometrics by Robert Edenborough. Published by Kogan Page, 1994.
Personality at Work by Adrian Furnham. Published by Routledge, 1992
Understanding Psychological Testing by Charles Jackson. Published by The British Psychological Society, 1996.
Intelligence: The Psychometric View by Paul Kline. Published by Routledge, 1990.
Personality: The Psychometric View by Paul Kline. Published by Routledge, 1993
The Handbook of Psychological Testing by Paul Kline. Published by Routledge, 1994
Modern Psychometrics: The Science of Psychological Assessment by John Rust and Susan Golombok. Published by Routledge, 1989.

A good general book on psychology, which contains details on the theory of psychological testing, is *Psychology: The Science of Mind and Behaviour* by Richard Gross (Hodder & Stoughton, 1992).

Finally, the most comprehensive range of books available in the UK which contain example test questions are published by Kogan Page.

Further Reading from Kogan Page

Creating Your Career, Simon Kent, 1997

Great Answers to Tough Interview Questions, 3rd edition, Martin John Yate, 1992

How to Choose a Career, 4th edition, Vivien Donald, 1996

How to Get the Top Jobs That are Never Advertised, Willet Weeks, 1996

How to Master Personality Questionnaires, Mark Parkinson, 1997

How to Pass Computer Selection Tests, Sanjay Modha, 1994

How to Pass Graduate Recruitment Tests, Mike Bryon, 1994

How to Pass Numeracy Tests, Harry Tolley and Ken Thomas, 1996.

How to Pass Selection Tests, Mike Bryon and Sanjay Modha, 1991

How to Pass Technical Selection Tests, Mike Bryon and Sanjay Modha, 1993

How to Pass the Civil Service Qualifying Tests, Mike Bryon, 1995

How to Pass the Police Initial Recruitment Test, Ken Thomas, Catherine Tolley and Harry Tolley, 1997

How to Pass Verbal Reasoning Tests, Harry Tolley and Ken Thomas, 1996

How You Can Get That Job!, Rebecca Corfield, 1992

Interviews Made Easy, Mark Parkinson, 1994

The Job Hunter's Handbook, David Greenwood, 1995

Job Hunting Made Easy, 3rd edition, John Bramham and David Cox, 1995

Preparing Your Own CV, Rebecca Corfield, 1990

Readymade CVs, Lynn Williams, 1996

Test Your Own Aptitude, 2nd edition, Jim Barrett and Geoff Williams, 1990

Your Readymade CV Action Kit (CD-ROM and book)

Index